A FUTURE
FOR FARM BUILDINGS

THE PUBLICATION OF THIS REPORT HAS BEEN GENEROUSLY SPONSORED BY
THE RURAL DEVELOPMENT COMMISSION, THE DEPARTMENT OF THE ENVIRONMENT AND
THE ERNEST COOK TRUST.

A Future for Farm Buildings is published by
SAVE Britain's Heritage, a registered charity
(no. 269129) founded in 1975 to campaign for historic
buildings at risk. Copies of this and other SAVE
publications are available from:

SAVE Britain's Heritage,
68 Battersea High Street,
London SW11 3HX.
Tel: 01-228 3336.

Printed September 1988.

© SAVE Britain's Heritage.

Edited by Sophie Andreae.

Designed by Jane Ewart.

ISBN 0 905978 26 9.

Printed by W. W. Hawes Printers Ltd., Elmswell, Suffolk.

A FUTURE
FOR FARM BUILDINGS

GILLIAN DARLEY

ACKNOWLEDGEMENTS

Above all, my thanks go to Kate Pugh who first took on this report, did the lion's share of the research but was unable, because of family commitments, to complete it. To some extent the debt that SAVE owes is reflected in the text. Some local authorities were outstandingly helpful in their responses; a few, I regret, were less than helpful. Inevitably, quotes and examples reflect those who co-operated, with often invaluable comments and first-hand experience of the issues involved. Similarly a number of other bodies, some National Parks, the National Trust and various leading firms of land agents were generous with their responses.

I would also like to thank David Collier of the NFU for all his help and advice, Rod Wild who has undertaken a survey of barns in Surrey and Philip Hughes of the Society for the Protection of Ancient Buildings. Thanks are due too to Ken Powell and to Marianne Watson-Smyth at the SAVE office and to Charlotte Scott-Barrett for help with picture research.

GILLIAN DARLEY.

Photographs are credited individually where they have not been taken by the author.

Photographs credited R.C.H.M.E. are reproduced by gracious permission of the Royal Commission on Historical Monuments (England).

CONTENTS

PART I

INTRODUCTION
8

FARM BUILDINGS TODAY
16

PART II

POLICY, LEGISLATION AND GRANTS
24

PLANNING POLICIES IN ACTION
34

PART III

DESIGN, CONSTRAINTS AND OPPORTUNITIES
44

EXAMPLES: TITHE BARNS
56

BARNS, LARGE MEDIUM AND SMALL
66

SUMMARY AND CONCLUSIONS
82

BIBLIOGRAPHY
84

The Great Barn of Abbotsbury Abbey, Dorset. Built c. 1400.

FOREWORD

Last year there were more applications to demolish listed barns than any other single building type. Indeed, taking barns and miscellaneous farm buildings together, they accounted for one in five of *all* applications for total demolition. These gloomy statistics have just been published – indeed as this report goes to press – in the English Tourist Board's *Heritage Monitor* for 1988. They clearly demonstrate the seriousness of the threat to a vital and yet under-appreciated part of the county's architectural heritage.

These figures do not take account, of course, of the many unlisted barns and farm buildings which are swept away each year unrecorded. Neither does it take account of the vast numbers that are crudely converted – many of them to houses – and in the process lose their essential character due to damaging alterations and additions and use of inappropriate materials. Deeply worrying is the number of listed barns which are now being "de-listed" following conversion to residential use. All too often, the conversion destroys the special architectural and historic interest for which the building was originally listed. Such an alternative use can hardly be said to constitute conservation.

The purpose of this report is to highlight this threat which has become all the more acute recently as farmers are urged to diversify and development pressures in many rural areas increase. It is also to illustrate what can be done in a positive and practical way. The report shows examples of barns which have been successfully rescued, some from virtual extinction like the magnificent twelfth century barn at Coggeshall in Essex. The vast cruck barn at Leigh Court, Worcestershire, is also now safe and undergoing a major repair programme with grant aid from English Heritage. Yet if these great tithe barns – the cathedrals among barns – can be at risk (and SAVE has just been notified of an application to demolish the Grade I listed barn at Waxham, Norfolk, illustrated on page 57) what chance is there for the lesser buildings, both listed and unlisted?

This report illustrates some of the many uses to which farm buildings can be put and urges that whilst barns are highly adaptable, conversion must respect the character and fabric of the original building. Many farm buildings can still be used within agriculture, a fact that is all too often overlooked.

The report discusses the varied sources of financial assistance for conversion projects and argues for a more coherent policy. It argues for the introduction of Rural Conservation Areas not just as a means of giving greater protection to buildings which form an integral part of many landscapes but as a way of providing assistance for repairs along the lines of Town Schemes in rural areas. At the moment, farm buildings fall through the net and are very seldom eligible for any historic buildings grant aid.

I would like to thank the sponsors of this book, the Rural Development Commission – which has done so much through its Council for Small Industries in Rural Areas to promote employment in converted farm buildings – the Department of the Environment and the Ernest Cook Trust for their help in making this publication possible.

SOPHIE ANDREAE
CHAIRMAN
SAVE BRITAIN'S HERITAGE

PART I
INTRODUCTION

The traditional farm buildings that are such a valuable, if threatened, aspect of the British landscape are a record of many strands of our history. They tell of social and economic life in the countryside, they record skills and demonstrate how the rich supply of building materials (much of it long gone) was used. They are often called 'vernacular' buildings and the reference to a common but regional language is an accurate one.

"Barns in their landscape are an index of regionalism . . . From them we can infer tradition, in architectural styles and craftsmanship; for example, regional and local economies, patterns of settlements and their changes through time . . . They form part of the landscape heritage in the fuller sense that they are also original evidence, the agrarian equivalents of the domestic and ecclesiastical evidence represented by manor and farm houses and by parish churches." The words are those of Peter Fowler,

FAR LEFT; Bransdale, North Yorkshire. A barn in the ownership of the National Trust. An unusual original feature is the dog kennel incorporated beneath the steps.

LEFT; Derelict oast houses, Worcestershire. Technological advances in the brewing industry – gas-fired kilns are now used to dry hops – have made the oast house a largely redundant building type. If these buildings are to survive as a familiar and beautiful feature of the landscape, new uses are essential.

THIS PAGE; Field barn, North Wales. In upland areas, where farming patterns have changed far less than in lowland regions, field barns like this are a common feature and are, indeed, an integral part of the landscape. A minimum degree of maintenance to these sturdy, stone-built structures will keep them watertight and prolong their life indefinitely.

former Secretary of the Royal Commission on Historical Monuments, in his essay in the SPAB Barns Book.[1]

Not only are these buildings valuable reminders of a traditional past, but they are also objects of great beauty within the landscape. Imagine it without them; the Downs shorn of the flint and chalk barns that are revealed on each turn of the folding hillsides, the Dales dull green valleys without the stone punctuation marks of countless field barns, even the increasingly featureless stretch of eastern and midland England without the huddled tiled or thatched roofs which often now rest in the shadow of grain silos and the new hangars of agricultural business. Now that the remorseless march to higher and higher productivity is checked, these buildings are not anachronistic left-overs – they are potentially useful structures, a resource which may find a use within agriculture or in dozens of other guises.

The examples illustrated later in this report are organised by building type, and so it is logical to follow the same pattern here. Obviously a building serving a particular purpose, say a tithe barn, will be determined by and will mirror the geology of the area so that a single building type will vary widely, region to region. In Lancashire, for example, there are massive stone-built tithe barns, disguising equally massive oak cruck frames, whilst their counterparts in East Anglia will be constructed from an oak frame put together on entirely different structural principles, its panels filled with lath and plaster, brick or even wattle. They both incorporate the threshing floors, the arrangements for ventilation, the vast transverse doors for entry and exit of waggons but in the matter of structure they are poles apart.

The decisive factor has always been the landscape; upland or lowland, determining two quite distinct agricul-

FAR LEFT; Manor Farm, East Quantoxhead, Somerset. Farm buildings, including large barns, cluster around the Manor House nearby, reflecting the ancient manorial pattern of a region of Britain where feudalism lingered late. This is a particularly fine example of the arrangement, with excellent use of traditional local building materials including thatch.

LEFT; Dovecote, Southrop, Gloucestershire. The dovecote at Southrop was built into the gable of a large barn, an economical and essentially functional arrangement which produces a pleasing composite structure (historical photograph).

ABOVE; Tarnbrook, Forest of Bowland, Lancs. Farm buildings group together to form a small self-contained hamlet. The individual buildings are typical of the region, but the ensemble is outstanding and the equivalent of a Conservation Area is needed to protect it.

tural patterns and from that, quite separate approaches to the design, grouping, siting and scale of traditional farm buildings. Climate, partially determined by the topography, has also played its part in traditional design; in the Lake District which can have up to three times the average annual rainfall of East Anglia, vernacular builders thought long and hard about shelter – a narrow line of slate roofing above the doors to the bank barn is evidence of the conclusion they reached. In every type of building, in every area of the country, some small accommodations were made to all such facts of life. The off-the-peg sheds of the mid twentieth century farming make no such regional adjustments; they are 'purpose made' but not in any specific fashion.

The location of the building, whether within the village or standing out in the fields, is an important clue to historic patterns of land ownership. The manorial pattern, with farms grouped within the village, often in the shadow of the church, is typical of those parts of the country where the feudal pattern lived on. Barns lining the village street are characteristic of much of the Midlands, and typical of many of the most beautiful stone-built areas of the country such as the Cotswolds and Northamptonshire. Villages here are a subtle blend of domestic buildings and functional, simple building types such as barns and cattle sheds.

Quite different is the disposition of farm buildings in, for example, much of East Anglia or Kent and Sussex where farmers were owner-occupiers from early days, the famous Tudor yeoman farmer of legend and reality. Here the farmhouse, and its contiguous buildings, stand far out of the

RIGHT; An upland farm in North Wales. Simple, economical buildings of local stone. The group consists, typically for this region, of a house and barn in a continuous range.

FAR RIGHT; Farm group in the Bredon Hills, Somerset. Sited in a valley bottom, the buildings – varied in date – are constructed of typical local materials.

BELOW; A typical bank barn in Cumbria. This is another composite building type, peculiar to the Lake District, which combines a hay barn above with a cowshed underneath (entered at a lower level). Hay from above is fed to the animals below. A large number of these buildings remain in use today – an example of the durability and practicality of many farm building types.

BELOW RIGHT; Model Farm, Kedleston, Derbyshire. This group of buildings is a careful piece of architectural design and has been ascribed to Robert Adam (who worked on the great house nearby). Not all farm buildings are "vernacular" in style – there are many farm buildings on great estates designed by major architects.

villages, centred in its acres.

Upland agriculture, based on cattle and sheep, offers another picture. Again farms are generally scattered across the landscape, but on a far smaller scale, giving a more intensive picture. From the far west of the country, in Cornwall (and the pattern is similar in Ireland, and, for that matter, in Brittany) to the Pennines, much of Wales and Scotland, this is a repeating picture only varied by the local stone and the use of whitewash in some areas, but not in others. Often the further subdivision of the land is marked by little field barns, one to a strip field, which stand in their hundreds along the valleys and dales of these areas. Then there are bank barns, which make use of the change of level. Hay is loaded into an upper level loft, to be fed down to the animals below (who enter from there). A simple stone structure, roofed in slate and sometimes with a slate 'pentice' roof to keep the farmer dry as he feeds the livestock, with characteristic protruding 'through stones', this is an example of a traditional farm building which has continued to serve its function and many are still in use.

The farmstead itself in these areas will be very compact, reflecting a relatively small acreage. The buildings, likely to be stone built, may be grouped around a yard, with midden,

LEFT; Tithe Barn, Hartpury, Gloucestershire. This is one of the grandest barns in the county, probably 14th century in date and built for the Abbey of Gloucester. It has a magnificent roof structure. The barn is still in a poor state of repair – as roof tiles become dislodged, a process which advances with each winter, the sturdy timbers beneath become gradually more saturated.

ABOVE; Cob construction, a mixture of clay, straw and grit. This is the building material of many barns in mid-Devon. Surprisingly, perhaps, a number have survived but buildings of this material are very vulnerable to neglect. If the thatch is allowed to deteriorate, water penetrates the walls which simply disintegrate.

and probably reflect the need of a farmer in these regions to be self-sufficient at times of year where severe weather might cut the family off for weeks at a time, together with livestock requiring winter fodder. Alternatively, the farm house and animal housing and crop storage may be built as one, the north country 'laith house', in which the lie of the land provides a natural drainage system.

To date, the upland farm buildings (field barns excepted) have fared better than their counterparts elsewhere. There are two reasons, one is that stone buildings, with their roofs maintained, are very sturdy and long-lived, the other is that agriculture in these regions has, until recently, seen far less change then elsewhere.

Although any building that is maintained, with a sound roof, clear gutters and solid walls, will withstand time, some materials are very vulnerable, once they become less well cared for and none more so than the regional variants on unfired earth building, whether 'clay bat' (mud bricks from East Anglia) or cob, the mixture of clay, straw and grit that forms the great majority of barns in mid Devon. A surprising number of these have survived, because they have had the traditional 'hat' and 'shoes', that is an overhanging roof and stone footings, but they are immensely vulnerable

ABOVE; Linhay, South Devon. A linhay is a typical regional building type. Stock are housed beneath, while hay is kept above. There is no reason to look at traditional farm buildings as an encumbrance. All over the country, thousands are still earning their keep on the farm. Buildings such as this have not survived because of sentiment, but because they serve and can continue to serve a purpose.

ABOVE RIGHT; Cruck Barn, Stonyhurst, Lancashire. This magnificent early structure, five bays long, is still very much in use for agriculture.

once the building has fallen into disrepair. Sometimes materials are mixed. The Devon 'linhay', a building which has an open fronted upper storey in which the hay is kept dry and aired, while the animals are cosily housed below, is a practical combination usually with cob walls (for warmth) but with slate supports and a strong timber structure. In East Anglia earth was packed into unfired bricks, mud pie fashion, and made a fine material for buildings which would be used to house livestock.

The farmstead, comprised of the house and its buildings, is the key element within the regional landscape of Britain. The buildings of the farmstead are divided between those designed originally for processing and storage, and those for the shelter and feeding of livestock.

Threshing barns can be many bays long or just a simple two bay affair with no more than a space to either side of the threshing floor. Large or small they have been redundant for at least one hundred years and have found themselves put to all manner of uses on the farm. A mixed farm would probably link the main barn with its animal housing, since the straw would be taken into cattle sheds or sties, whilst the manure or slurry would be collected nearby for ease of transport to the fields. In fact the traditional farmstead has the beauty of function being the absolute determinant of its form.

New buildings, and building types, were introduced in step with the march of progress and to reflect the increasing complexity and scale of agriculture. Some areas, especially those where the Agricultural Revolution of the late 18th century marched on with greatest force, are dotted with auxiliary buildings; cattle sheds and barns which serve vast estates, for which a single central farmstead would have been quite impracticable. Estates such as the Holkham estate in North Norfolk are a network of farmsteads and far flung foldyards, which with mechanisation have little practical use.

A traditional barn, for example, often has a wheel or engine house built onto one side, to power the threshing process once the flail and the winnower were replaced by more efficient and less labour-intensive methods. Often buildings combined function, so that the hay was stored overhead, the animals lodged beneath, or a granary, safe from predators was located overhead in the cartshed.

Change in the function of these buildings often came without fuss; harrows, ploughs and trailers could tuck into the cartshed, pallets moved by neatly mobile fork lift trucks are

stored in the old barns and so on, as the crops and equipment changed over the years. Many farmers needed a range of new buildings, designed to particular specifications, but many of those same farmers found the old buildings still worked well. Turkeys flourished in one solidly built barn, suckling calves in another. A small scale milking parlour could be slotted into a barn, while the handling and storage of new 'crops' – timber for example – could be done just as well in the existing buildings, for the cost of maintaining the roof and gutters.

There is no reason to look at traditional farm buildings as an encumbrance. All over the country, it is clear that thousands are still earning their keep on the farm. Sometimes they are all that is needed, sometimes they have been extended with ranges of new buildings, in the same way that pre-nineteenth century buildings were added to and altered with the coming of mechanisation. The vernacular farm buildings that still make up a remarkable part of the rural architectural inheritance have not survived because of sentiment, but because they did the job well enough. That remains the case, and with the changes in policy and attitude that we describe later in this book the future may be brighter, with grant aid and assistance to see the traditional buildings of the countryside take centre stage in a rural revival.

Field Barn in Derbyshire. This is typical of those which have been converted successfully as "stone tents" for walkers. Originally used for storing hay in upland fields, these buildings are remarkably solidly constructed and a modest expenditure on maintenance gives them a prolonged life in a useful new function. The Derbyshire Peak District without its traditional field barns would be a far less interesting landscape.

FARM BUILDINGS TODAY

There is nothing new about redundant farm buildings. Many of our finest barns have already been redundant for a century or more. Farmers have long been used to altering and adapting their existing buildings in answer to changing circumstances. John Woodforde quotes Arthur Young's comment that Suffolk barns were 'uselessly large' and that was in 1810.

Technology has been the main agent of change, from the advent of the threshing machine onwards, but there have been changes in farming practice, too, which have played their part. The different theories of animal husbandry, such as the recent practice of housing sheep in winter months, the increasing productivity of the land leading to the need for secure storage, such as grain silos, introduction of vegetable crops grown on large scale and which require packing and storage, have all had an impact on the existing buildings of the farm. Machinery has on the one hand become larger, too large for all but the most massive barns, on the other, much more adaptable to confined spaces, in the form of fork-lift trucks which can turn on a penny piece.

Shifts in policy and emphasis, now determined from Brussels, have led the modern agricultural revolution. The difference between this and earlier revolutions in the countryside, has been one of pace. With the European Community's Common Agricultural Policy, and its anomalies, as the agent of change, farmers have been facing uncertainty to such an extent that there is no assurance that what I am writing now will reflect the position in even six months' time. Almost any upheaval, from exceptional harvests to currency movement, can affect agricultural affairs. The EEC, now including the less sophisticated farm practices of the Mediterranean countries, will continue as a bulwark but with less profligacy.

Farm amalgamation, the trend in the 1960s and 1970s, left enormous numbers of redundant farm buildings surplus to requirements. For owners of large estates, such as the National Trust (Reading Report para. 3.114)[2] the position arose that while farmhouses and cottages increased in value, and became increasingly sought after, farm buildings – possibly adjacent – have been uneconomic to maintain, suffer from disuse or under use and represent a wasting asset. In

possibility, pointed out in the NFU fact sheet on redundant farm buildings,[4] that the farmer may be approached by a potential tenant. CoSIRA also keeps lists of those searching for premises.

That change in agriculture and the rural economy will at last benefit the historic buildings of the countryside is beyond doubt. In the last few years the future of historic farm buildings has become a prime conservation issue. The Society for the Protection of Ancient Buildings initiated a new level of public interest with a 'Barns Day' held in 1980, following it up with a nation-wide survey, the Domesday Report, the results of which are being analysed at the moment. Volunteers took on a parish at a time, recording the state of barns and farm buildings as they found them. Although only a few counties were covered comprehensively, an enormous amount of information has been gathered and, perhaps, as important, a vast reservoir of public concern for the future of farm buildings was tapped.

The British Tourist Authority published 'Britain's Historic Buildings: a policy for their future use', (known as the Montagu Report after its Chairman Lord Montagu) in 1980. In rec-

the case of the Trust their vernacular buildings have become a major concern. They have been carrying out a national survey of their properties, as well as promoting traditional methods and skills in their repair. Their stated aim is to keep the buildings in agricultural use if at all possible, and if not, to consider residential use as the last resort. They are prepared to divert resources to fulfil their responsibilities in this direction, sharing the cost of maintenance with their tenants.

Farm income has declined 36% in real terms since 1970 (Gretton Report)[3] and the search for alternative sources of income has become increasingly urgent. Part-time farming has, on the other hand, been on a steady increase and the 1987 MAFF Annual Review of Agriculture reports a rise of 7½% between 1984 and 1987 alone. This seems to reflect the diversification that government and its agencies are so keen to promote.

These changes are potentially good news for the existing historic and traditional agricultural buildings of the countryside, because they represent a potential resource, an asset on which to build. It is quicker and often cheaper, to seize the advantage of a building on the spot than to enter the lengthy and expensive business of buying or building a new building. In addition planning policies are more favourable to conversion, in many cases, than to new build.

As farmers move beyond the strict confines of agriculture and are being encouraged into different forms of exploiting the countryside, its products and attractions, they have to become conversant with the world of marketing and sales, which includes seizing the potential of the buildings which are already there. New moves towards non-capital grant aid will help supply this more sophisticated approach. Although the onus to act may be on the farmer, there is also the

FAR LEFT; Colesbourne, Gloucestershire. This early 19th century stone-built barn is still in full use for the storage of crops.

LEFT; Meifod, Powys. The fine barns at Dyffryn form two sides of a courtyard. They are timber-framed and infilled with brick and probably date from c. 1800. The combination of materials is typical of the Borders.

THIS PAGE; These barns in North Norfolk are typical of the practices of the great Georgian and Victorian estates. Barns and foldyards were needed at strategic points on the farm.

RIGHT; Derelict. The horse-powered wheelhouses of Northern England form another totally redundant building type. They can only survive in the long term in a new use. This example has now been converted to arts use in a new town.

FAR RIGHT; Derelict. Paulton, Gloucestershire. If roofs are not maintained, walls will not stand long.

BELOW; Derelict. Church Farm, Rollesby, Norfolk.

BELOW RIGHT; Derelict. Field Barn, Cumbria. It would make an ideal "stone tent".

It was the Farm Capital Grants Scheme of 1957 which encouraged the vast investment in new farm buildings. This led to the sweeping away of many traditional buildings and the dereliction of many more. Grant aid was pumped into the construction of new buildings but no equivalent funding was provided for repairs to existing buildings. The Ministry of Agriculture, Fisheries and Food (MAFF) gave no advice on maintenance or conversion to new agricultural uses and this simply exacerbated the problem.

ent years there has been a spate of publications, as well as national, regional and local awards (run by bodies such as the Country Landowners' Association, the Council for the Protection of Rural England, and CoSIRA) and conferences which have all sustained and encouraged interest in the subject.

At the same time that a wide selection of bodies with an interest in rural policy have entered the ring, so too a more developed interest in the background to the subject has helped to inform the debate. Vernacular building studies and groups are proliferating. The Historic Farm Buildings Group [5] was formed in 1985 as a result of the volume of interest and takes care in its newsletters and annual reports to keep abreast of the whole subject of reuse and the future for traditional farm buildings – a healthy marriage between scholarship and practicality. Local groups too, such as the Devon Buildings Group, provide regional expertise and pressure at a time when the local authorities are more hard-pressed and sometimes desperately lacking in appropriate expertise or interest.

Latterly too, the Ministry of Agriculture Fisheries and Food has responded to the change in climate and regional conferences for surveyors and ADAS officers now include the subject of traditional farm buildings – which cannot any longer be ignored. But there is a bitter tinge to this late awakening, for it was the Farm Capital Grants Scheme of 1957 which precipitated the vast new building programme, often needlessly and regrettably sweeping away buildings which might be more practical for modern farm use and diversification than the lightweight, off the peg structures that rose on their ashes.

Traditional farm buildings – this one now with a modern corrugated iron roof – are still functional and provide warm and comfortable accommodation for stock. In recent years, interest in traditional buildings has grown – vernacular building studies groups are proliferating and bodies such as the Country Landowners' Association, the Council for the Protection of Rural England and CoSIRA have all encouraged this growth. The MAFF is at last beginning to respond: regional conferences for surveyors and ADAS officers now include the subject of traditional farm buildings.

Even after the incursions of neglect, the tally of historic farm buildings remains remarkable. In Essex, which has 13,500 listed buildings, 1,700 of these were agricultural structures and over 1,000 barns. There may well be many more still unlisted but of historic value. On the evidence of a sample taken from the SPAB Domesday Survey, covering 48 barns in seven parishes, the comments on condition listed 40% as good, 37% as fair and the rest poor.

The twentieth century fate of historic farm buildings can be divided into three phases. After the severe effect upon agricultural investment during and between the two World Wars, the state of agriculture was so depressed that virtually no capital had gone into new buildings, or for more than basic maintenance of existing buildings.

In the post war period, Government support for agriculture, with its insistence on self sufficiency as a goal, pumped money into grant aiding a programme of new buildings. The opposite side of the coin was neglect of old buildings, which attracted no MAFF grant aid, no advice on their maintenance or conversion to new agricultural uses, and merely exacerbated the problem. Adverse tax and grant systems created an unfavourable financial balance between investment in repair and new construction.

Regional building skills, based on familiarity with local materials, were being lost and so breeze block replaced stone, corrugated iron replaced tile or thatch. Even so, buildings botched could be rescued; buildings flattened were no so fortunate.

THE CASE FOR CONSERVATION

Why don't we just admit that historic farm buildings have no part to play in the countryside outside the Open Air Museum? The truth is that a vast, if depleted, number remain in agricultural use (even if an adaptation far removed from their original func-

Grange Barn, Coggeshall, Essex. Although in good condition after the war, this outstanding mid-12th century barn was neglected – in the midst of a working farmyard and by 1980 it had virtually collapsed. Only the late intervention of local authority and national funding saved it.

tion) for the reason that they are a valuable resource, and, often are strong competition for the off the peg sheds and purpose built structures which have been introduced in the last thirty-odd years. Often enough, a traditional building offers ideal conditions. Take the care of young animals. Calves need well-insulated quarters in the early stages. Masonry or brick walls will provide immeasurably better conditions than any modern alternative. Equally, for both animals and crop storage the kind of ventilation offered by weatherboarded walls or pantiled (or tiled) roofs is hard to match with inexpensive lightweight modern materials.

As the pressure for nature conservation has risen, and with it, government intervention to preserve traditional farming methods for landscape reasons, there is a very strong argument for the buildings in the scene. A traditional landscape devoid of traditional buildings would be shorn of much of its appeal. Although the new government support system for a limited number of Environmentally Sensitive Areas (ESAs) does not specifically target the buildings in that area, it contains a measure of support for their continued maintenance.

No one should presume, either, that any building whatsoever is safe. As recently as 1980 the Grange Barn, Coggeshall, recognised as a medieval monastic barn of national and international importance with timbers dating from the mid 12th century had all but collapsed. In the middle of a prosperous looking working farmyard, it lurched to extinction. Only the late intervention of local authority and national funding saved it. More recently still, English Heritage have allotted a considerable sum to the spectacular cruck barn at Leigh, in Worcestershire, relatively well maintained by its owners but far beyond their means to restore and care for. The great tithe barns have always been a special case; the National Trust bears responsibility (if not ownership) for a number, and local authorities own other examples. Nevertheless, there are still buildings which outflank the parish church for splendour and dimensions for which an individual owner still bears responsibility. This is a category for which the public purse has frequently been opened, but the vast majority of owners of traditional farm buildings cannot resort so easily to that source of funding.

One of the main justifications for urgent action in the matter of redundant farm buildings is the current unhappy climate in which development control and conservation policy have to be carried out. As we see later in the report the rapid increase in the number of successful appeals, 41% and rising, the changes in the framework of planning and an anti-interventionist climate are hazardous obstacles in the way. Conversion of farm buildings is going on apace, but

all too often, to the wrong use and without adequate attention to either design or materials.

The government is highly encouraging towards the conversion of farm buildings. "It is perfectly proper that new industries be in the countryside and jobs are returning. It means new uses for old barns". Those sentiments, voiced by the then Minister of State for Agriculture, John Selwyn Gummer, at a Suffolk Preservation Society seminar, "The Countryside faced with change" held in autumn 1987, are ample proof that government thinking supports the tenor of this report.

Alternative use has been the saviour of many a historic building, from country house to church, from railway station to textile factory. Initial scepticism in many cases has changed to a recognition of possibilities; the last fifteen years of conservation action bear testimony to the shift of attitude. That old buildings represent an economic resource has been argued hard, and slowly accepted by example. Central to the exercise must be a new use which can stimulate sufficient investment to repair and convert the building and thereafter, produce adequate capital to maintain the building. But in the rush of advice and apparent glimpses of financial assist-

Cruck Barn, Leigh Court, Worcestershire. Although relatively well-maintained, this **outstanding cruck barn, a cathedral among barns,** had become a burden to its owners and there was no appropriate alternative use in sight for such an exceptional structure. Last year, **English Heritage** took this barn into guardianship and will open it to the public in 1989.

Coombeshead Farm, Arlington, near Barnstable, Devon. A building such as this one (owned by the National Trust) does not readily lend itself to conversion for housing. The National Trust's survey of farm buildings in its care has led to a new recognition of vernacular buildings in that organisation.

ance, it is easy to overlook the point of the exercise; the retention of the building, as near as possible in its traditional form. The 'fine print' of conversion, the quality of the job, from the overall design to the authenticity of the materials, is liable to be overlooked in the rush to find a solution. Yet if a conversion has the effect of entirely remodelling the building, leaving nothing of its character, inside or out, then the exercise of preservation was in vain.

But the rate of change in agriculture is such that planning authorities, granting permission for a conversion, have to consider whether there will be a demand for replacement buildings for farm purposes, once the building in question has been taken out of agricultural use. As the Reading Report notes (para. 3.38) "deciding what is redundant is clearly crucial since it may be that the building is no longer used because the farming type has changed or the farm has ceased trading. This may be a relatively temporary change in response to current economic circumstances, but once the building is converted, the change may be irreversible".

Redundant farm buildings suggest a major possibility to extend the range of activities and economic opportunities in small rural communities. The Rural Development Commission or its counterparts in Wales and Scotland has fully recognised this and increasingly, can point to examples of successes to encourage the fainter hearts.

A working oast-house outside Smarden, Kent. The picture in the centre shows the inside of the "cowl", which provided the draught needed to dry the hops. This oast-house has now been converted to use gas for drying. This illustrates that new technology can be used in an old building.

ABOVE; In a few instances, the only way to save a building is to move it to a new site but this must be a last resort.

RATE OF LOSS

Much of the recent research work has been carried out in a race against time; although figures are available only in certain counties and related to listed buildings, the increase in planning applications for listed building consent to demolish or change use speak for themselves. (See Table on p. 40). Dereliction and demolition have already taken their toll and not all surviving buildings have fared well at the hands of the converters, hence the rising numbers of de-listed barns.

There is no nationwide picture available, but certain surveys have pointed up interesting points. A MAFF research exercise showed a surprisingly high level of continued use of traditional farm buildings, if only for storage and outhousing purposes.

But even surveys which show the extent of loss of known listed farm buildings, or of the current use and state of remaining examples, can be diverted by all manner of local factors. For example in affluent areas of the south east and East Anglia many farmhouses have been sold out of the farm long since, taking a barn or two with them. Usually in such cases the barn remains unconverted, used as a storage shed, playroom, garage or similar, but at the same time cannot be considered (for purposes of survey) as an agricultural building.

1 SPAB, *Barns Book,* Conference Report, 1982.
2 University of Reading, *Redundant Farm Buildings: Alternative Uses in the Remoter Rural Areas of England and Wales,* 1987.
3 *Gretton Report,* County Landowners' Association, 1985.
4 NFU, *Redundant Farm Buildings,* June, 1988.
5 Historic Farm Buildings Group, *Annual Report.*

PART II
POLICY, LEGISLATION AND GRANTS

HISTORIC BUILDINGS GRANT AID

In many respects farm buildings are the poor relations of the architectural heritage. Because of the relative ease of defining the scale of the problem, and the quality of their architecture, country houses, churches and many other categories of historic building are the constant concern of many bodies. Unfortunately even some of the most important farm buildings in the country have fallen by the wayside; protected neither by their owners, nor by the intervention of public authorities. Less easily recognised than medieval domestic architecture, many humble exteriors disguise interiors of staggering beauty, craftsmanship and age. Yet despite recent improvements from the countrywide re-listing, they are far from fully protected under the statutory powers available, and when they are

FAR LEFT; Attention to detail and quality of craftsmanship are evident in this simple functional building in the Lancashire Pennines.

LEFT; Chalk and flint are used with imagination on this barn in the Thames Valley. This barn is still in agricultural use. Grade II listed buildings in rural areas are seldom eligible for historic buildings grants. In order to qualify buildings need to be either individually "outstanding" or situated within a Conservation Area. Most Conservation Areas are in towns: there is a real need to extend the concept of the Conservation Area and its system of grant aid to the countryside.

THIS PAGE; A Victorian model farm in Essex. Farm buildings like this were the consequence of the 19th century agricultural expansion and the introduction of machinery. Ranges of buildings like this can readily be converted to light industrial use without destroying their character.

adequately listed, they often meet with continued dereliction or destruction by default – in the shape of appalling conversions.

While it is important to survey the policies and grant aid available under the various headings that follow, from the Ministry via various government agencies concerned with the revitalisation and regeneration of the countryside, it is essential to realise that the simple granting of consent for conversion, grant aided or not, is not necessarily the rescue of a redundant farm building. It may well be its death – as a recognisable, functional, rural building. In the illustrations that accompany the report, we hope that quality will make its own point.

The funds available for grant aid to listed buildings, from sources specifically concerned with historic buildings *per se,* are meagre (see SAVE's report, Conservation: A Credit Account, 1988) [6]. Nor is obtaining such grant aid straight forward, even in the cases of the most exceptional structures.

When the NFU presented its evidence to the House of Commons Environmental Committee, in spring 1986, it was strongly critical of arrangements for financial assistance of maintenance and repair works to historic buildings. The comments of David Collier, from that organisation's Land Use Section are worth quoting at length, for little has changed. "The present arrangements for the public funding of historic building repairs might with some justification be described as shambolic and inadequate. Shambolic because grants and loans are theoretically available from a long list of authorities and organisations, under a range of statutes – many of them not specifically aimed at historic buildings – and offered subject to satisfaction of disparate criteria. Inadequate because budgets are too meagre; only buildings of the very finest quality attract

Church Farm, Rollesby, Norfolk. This farm was in the ownership of the County Council but has now been passed to the Norfolk Historic Buildings Trust. Part of the complex is medieval and listed Grade I. Whilst workshop use would be more desirable, as it would involve far less alteration, the Trust – which acts as a revolving fund – finds itself forced to consider a residential solution in order to cover the costs of repairs.

satisfactory rates of grant; and little if any account is taken of the extraordinary cost of repair in traditional materials or of the utility of the building when restored". Discussing the latter, Mr. Collier continues, "As a rule of thumb, we would consider that the grant aid in respect of a given building should be equal to the difference between the cost of repairs in modern and traditional materials with an allowance in respect of the usefulness of the building to its owner as opposed to the public".

The amount of money available from central and local government sources for repairing the fabric of historic farm buildings, regardless of function, is minimal. English Heritage and its predecessor, the Historic Buildings Council, have offered financial assistance towards a tiny handful of outstanding barns in recent years. The National Heritage Memorial Fund has helped finance repair work through low interest loans of three historic farm buildings during its eight years of existence. Local authority conservation is at the sharp end of staff reductions and the financial squeeze. A bias towards urban conservation, with Town Schemes and Conservation Areas, has always made the going harder for those arguing for aid for farm buildings. Local building preservation trusts tend to work on a

Leighterton, Gloucestershire. County Councils frequently own farms. They should aim to set an example in the treatment of their property.

When these barns in the hamlet of Leighterton ceased to be used for agricultural purposes in 1986, Gloucestershire County Council immediately sought permission for residential conversion. The Society for the Protection of Ancient Buildings objected on the grounds that a more imaginative approach to reuse might conserve the historic buildings better.

rolling basis and therefore have to look for projects which will sell on with least difficulty. Church Farm Rollesby, in Norfolk, belonged to the County Council. It has now been passed on to the Norfolk Historic Buildings Trust who find that the only economic solution is a residential conversion, which for a Grade I listed farm building is far from ideal.

Gloucester County Council, owners of a number of barns in the village of Leighterton, applied in 1986 to convert them all to residential use. If the County or District Council does not set an example, both by its willingness to act and propose suitable future uses for a barn or farmstead, the argument is that much harder to sustain when private developers' planning proposals seek to question the council's stated policy. At the same time, as a County formulates a policy it frequently finds that no simple approach can be applied district to district; in Norfolk the circumstances are utterly different in, for example, North Norfolk where tourism exerts enormous pressure, and other districts where rural decline is much starker and the need for employment and diversification far more pressing.

Architectural Heritage Fund loans have helped to ensure a future for the Great Barn Avebury, now used as a Study Centre, and for the Grange

Cartshed, Burnham Thorpe, Norfolk. This is a traditional building type which still provides useful shelter for farm machinery – all that is required is regular maintenance.

Barn, Coggeshall. Loans provide a useful topping up function, but are only available against buildings of very exceptional architectural and historic significance.

However the anomalous situation pointed out by Michael Pearce in his report for SAVE, 'Conservation: A Credit Account' is constantly undermining any structure of grants, or loan finance. To begin with the vast majority of listed buildings are not eligible for grant at all, and in the case of farm buildings they are rarely sited within a Conservation Area in order to qualify under that heading. Pearce argues for tax incentives (on the model of the US and Netherlands) and for the abolition, or failing that, lowering of the rate of VAT on repairs to old buildings. That crippling burden, often consuming the entire grant offered on an historic building, is one more disincentive for the retention of traditional farm buildings.

The essential tool for a local authority hoping to ensure a future for threatened listed buildings is a knowledge of the situation. Buildings at risk registers should be an essential tool, and Essex County Council's valuable publications, first a general list and second, one devoted to agricultural structures, point the way. Such a publicly available register has a number of functions; it allows the conservation section of the Council to have an available check-list, for consultation as soon as an application comes in. It is available for potential tenants or buyers who may be able to provide a future for the building (and the first list has already identifiably saved almost forty buildings), and offers a quick check on condition. (Essex, in common with a number of southern and eastern counties, was devastated following the hurricane of October 1987 and a depressing number of farm buildings are described as dilapidated by "act of nature"). At the end of the introduction, the Council makes its views clear. "The County Council's historic buildings and conservation team will readily provide advice to anyone wishing to seek a solution to the problems mentioned above, including low cost remedial repairs in appropriate situations. It must be remembered, however, that the preferred future for such structures will always be that which continues their agricultural use".

MINISTRY OF AGRICULTURE

The policies which affect historic farm buildings fall into the area of concern of the Ministry of Agriculture as well as that of the Department of the Environment. Rural policy is something of a tug-of-war, with other agencies such as the Rural Development Commission and its counterparts in Wales and Scotland making the running – but without the resources to be fully effective. Many would accept that the demarcation disputes between ministries and the ineffective levels of funding of other agencies, have exacerbated the already mounting problems of rural areas. The Country Landowners' Association in their Steele Addison Report [7] referred to this, the recent publication, A Rural Strategy, [8] published by Rural Voice, cited an integrated approach to policies as an essential ingredient towards the future well-being of the countryside, whilst a recent article in The Economist (13.2.88) carried a swingeing attack on the present state of affairs. It pointed out that "MAFF has had the power to give grant-aid for diversification since mid-1986, and has yet to hand out a penny". The article placed its faith in a strengthened, and properly financed Rural Development Commission with strong regional offices, on the model of the mid Wales or Scottish highlands development agencies.

The Economist criticism is the more unfortunate in the face of government efforts to present information in a unified package. In March 1987 it launched ALURE, (Alternative Land Uses and Rural Employment) which followed the example of a Welsh equivalent, presented in 1986 and titled DRIVE (Development of Rural Initiative, Venture and Enterprise) – the first integrated source of information. The CPRE response to ALURE was a "fear... that the major casualty of the Government's new vision of the countryside is the role of strategic planning". They see the new direction as the encouragement of "a range of new options... being made available on a sporadic and *ad hoc* basis to farmers and rural dwellers, in the rather pious hope that these will somehow be able to cope with the problems of agricultural surpluses and provide new jobs and incomes, while protecting the countryside".

In the past the entire thrust of MAFF grant aid was to increase productivity and to boost farmers' incomes, and envisaged no role for historic buildings within the working farmstead. The old system of capital grants positively encouraged the demolition and effectively enforced the dereliction of traditional farm buildings in favour of new, purpose-built structures. That so many survive, against the odds and without grant aid or encouragement for their adaptation, speaks for itself.

The low priority accorded to the fate of traditional farm buildings is characterised in comments made by a north western planning authority. Tameside Metropolitan Borough, in a letter to SAVE last year, addressing the potential of keeping agricultural buildings in use, found little support from the Ministry. "The major prolems arise when there is a partial existing or potential agricultural use, which is not, however, of sufficient economic worth to justify the costs involved in the proper repair and maintenance of very large buildings. The attitude of MAFF is rarely helpful if retention of the building in agricultural use is the aim, in that they appear to view their role as supporting modern methods of working. Possibly the recent emphasis on reducing production may lead to some amelioration of this view".

Now, the realisation that instead of an unremitting race for self sufficiency the CAP requires land to be taken out of cultivation, has opened up new uncertainties. Historic farm buildings are not exempt from any of this. Set-aside schemes or reduced price support have enormous implications. Just one adjustment, the introduction of dairy quotas in April 1984 jeopardised farm incomes in many parts of the country – particularly in the south west of England or west Wales where many farms were solely dairying enterprises. To diversify from that basis required strong nerve and imagination – although as the examples show, it happened. Alterations in the beef support scheme will also take their toll as well as major adjustments to lower the cereals surplus. Farmers who had taken vast bank loans to invest in new buildings or plant, often installed in existing, older buildings, found themselves against the wall. Those who did so in order to modernize their farming practice, and are now being encouraged (and paid) to return to old practices, are puzzled - to say the least.

The shift in agricultural policy is echoed by the changes in emphasis of the grant system. For example, the Powy Digest published by ADAS in the issue August 1988, comments existing buildings and facilities should be considered for use or adaptation, but adds, "Will their use detract from the performance of, or interfere with the running of, existing enterprises?". New grant schemes underline the diversification of agricultural enterprises, and include recognition of landscape conservation considerations, almost but not quite, at the expense of the built environment. Certainly the efficacy of the nature conservation lobby should be a lesson to those arguing for the economic and physical survival of traditional rural buildings.

Barn, Worcestershire. A functional brick building providing valuable storage space. MAFF should consider grants for the repair and maintenance of traditional buildings. In the past, capital grants were only available for the construction of new buildings. Recent shifts in agricultural policy provides the opportunity for reconsideration of this type of approach.

THIS PAGE; Hendra Farm, St. Ives, Cornwall. New economic uses on the farm can help fund the repair of historic farm buildings. This range of buildings, formerly derelict, have been converted (with the help of a Rural Development Commission grant) to provide studios for a number of design-based businesses.

OPPOSITE PAGE; Acres Farm, Bradfield, Berkshire. The repair and conversion of this characteristic thatched barn was grant-aided by the Rural Development Commission.

The Farm Land and Rural Development Bill will widen the capital grant scheme to cover the country, and widens the range of projects. In addition, non-capital grants are proposed. These will be offered to farmers who wish to investigate the viability of farm-related business and to commission feasibility studies, market research and the marketing of products and services. For the former two, a 50% grant is proposed, for the latter a 30% grant with a ceiling of £2,000 for individuals and £5,000 for groups. The Agriculture Act 1986 allows for capital grants within farming while an amendment, announced in November 1987, offers grants for diversification. The Agricultural Improvement Scheme enables a farmer to receive grants of 25% on investments up to £24,000 in tourism, crafts or light industry. Limited to the Less Favoured Areas (which constitute 44% of agricultural land in England and 60% in Wales and a total of 53% of agricultural land in the UK) these ventures must be linked to approved farm improvement plans. The grants can also be applied to the repair of buildings in continuing agricultural use if this can be shown to increase productivity, again within an improvement plan. This is the first time that MAFF capital grants have been directed towards traditional farm buildings under any heading whatsoever.

Thus, farmers are being encouraged to widen the basis of their incomes by the offer of grants towards farm tourism and recreation enterprises in the Less Favoured Areas and through its advisory service ADAS, throughout the rest of England and Wales. For all these agencies, conservation is not the primary purpose of the exercise, but nevertheless a beneficiary of valuable funds.

Conservation grants from MAFF cover the provision, replacement or improvement of hedges, walls built of traditional materials with their associated gates, stiles and footbridges, trees and shelter belts can be obtained at a basic rate of 30% or 60% in the LFAs. Not so long ago, grant aid for drainage and rationalisation programmes facilitated the removal of these same features, as hefty grants towards new buildings speeded the demise of traditional farm buildings in the 1950s and 60s.

The designation of Environmentally Sensitive Areas was the main achievement of the nature conservation movement, beginning with eight designated areas and now extended to twelve in England and Wales and five in Scotland. The Countryside Commission recommendations presented to the Minister of Agriculture and the Secretary of State for Wales (April 1986) also contained some comment on the limitations of designation, including the importance of vernacular buildings which are often not in agricultural use or under the control of the farmer or tenant. Nevertheless those buildings which fall naturally within the ambit of the scheme are not necessarily beneficiaries of a system which has been developed to protect traditional forms of cultivated, and wild, landscape and within which buildings are seen as incidentals. This would make better sense of they were afforded dependable protection and funding from elsewhere, such as the Department of the Environment, as in the urban environment, within Conservation Areas. The buildings of the countryside in many ways fall between stools.

The protection afforded to landscape, in the form of National Parks, AONBs and ESAs (see above), administered by MAFF, has far outstripped that given to traditional farm buildings – within the same areas. The

bodies which argue for landscape, the CPRE and its Welsh counterpart, the Countryside Commission and the Nature Conservancy Council are concerned with the use of and access to the countryside; pressure in this direction has led to an estimated one-third of the land area of the UK being protected in some fashion. Compare the fact that only 2% of all buildings are listed, and of these, only a tiny fraction of them are farm buildings and the inequity of the situation is obvious.

RURAL DEVELOPMENT COMMISSION

It is the Rural Development Commission which offers the best future to redundant farm buildings. All the lobbyists for the countryside recognise that this body is desperately under-funded for the scope of work it has been set up to do. The Rural Development Commission constitutes the Government's main advisory body on the economic and social development of rural England. It aims to strengthen the economy of rural areas particularly by increasing the number and variety of employment opportunities as well as ensuring their corollaries, housing and social and community facilities and amenities. Most of its resources are concentrated on providing premises in designated Rural Development Areas either by building advance workshops through its agency, English Estates or the local authority, or through grants offered by the Council for Small Industries in Rural Areas (CoSIRA). Launched in 1983, the Redundant Buildings Grant Scheme contributes 25% of the cost of conversion. In 1987 it was extended to 'tourist and associated leisure projects', recognising the increasingly

Acres Farm, Bradfield, Berkshire. This barn is now in light industrial use. A manufacturer of brass fenders and other household fittings finds it ideal accommodation. A new structure has been erected inside as a precaution against fire.

6 SAVE Britain's Heritage, *Conservation: A Credit Account*, Michael Pearce, 1988.
7 *Steele Addison Report*, County Landowners' Association, 1984.
8 Rural Voice, *A Rural Strategy*, October 1987.
9 *Gretton Report*, County Landowners' Association, 1985.

important contribution which such businesses make to employment in rural areas'. CoSIRA also offers loan finance in certain cases.

The newest Rural Development Commission schemes echo some of the MAFF grant schemes. The grants for Marketing Consultancy and Exhibition are provided by the Department of Employment; they are offered at 50% up to a ceiling of £1,000 for the former and £500 for the latter. There is also a new partnership scheme, aiming to attract in private sector finance and called ACCORD (Assistance for Co-ordinated Rural Development). The Scottish Development Agency established a Rural Projects and Initiatives Unit in November 1985 and one of its most successful arms in the DRAW scheme (Development of Rural Area Workshops) offering 25% of project costs (excluding purchase) up to £15,000. The take-up was so heavy that it was topped up twice in 1986. Similar schemes are available in Wales.

However, Rural Development Areas tend to correspond closely to the Less Favoured Areas, and this means that there are many equally hard hit farming areas covered by neither category. Lines on maps make convenient cut-off points for the bureaucrat but make little sense to someone who discovers that because of an arbitrary decision, they are excluded from all the advantages available to a neighbour. Outside the RDAs, CoSIRA offers a wide range of advisory services, but no capital grand aid.

THE PROBLEMS

Most grants that have been discussed above are nothing more than pump-priming, and certainly do not ensure the rescue of disused farm buildings in themselves. Farmers are, in general, conservative creatures and even with the promise of considerable financial reward do not rush into things: one East Anglian land agent, quoted in the *Financial Times* property pages recently, noted that "there is a tendency for farmers to feel that, if they keep their heads down, the problems will blow away".

In one rural development study, carried out at Monyash in the Peak District, aimed at creating new business opportunities, new community institutions and improving the village environment, a particularly favourable grant scheme still failed to encourage farmers to put their redundant farm buildings to new use, in spite of the success of one overnight camping barn in the village. With so many other concerns, more closely connected with the business of agriculture, farmers in the late 1980s are unlikely to have the time and energy to explore options outside their usual sphere of activity. Publicity for new ventures in the farming press, local newspapers or advice from ADAS officers would all assist in this. But the main obstacle remains the enormously unwieldy, and diffuse, and inadequate, system of grants.

INCENTIVES AND AWARDS

As part of a general heightening of awareness of the importance of quality in the conversion and maintenance of traditional farm buildings, a wide range of competitions both within the agriculture and architectural/environmental categories are now held and tend to attract good publicity, both locally and nationally. They prove an excellent way of promoting imaginative solutions and putting good ideas into circulation.

The Royal Welsh Agricultural Society promotes its Countryside Caretakers Award, set up in 1983, and the 1987 award, it stated, would be given to "the person whose work in the restoration of old farm buildings combines landscape conservation, imagination, architecture and enterprise most effectively." They used the occasion of the award presentation to be quite critical of standards and quality of workmanship which makes a useful combination of carrot and stick.

The CLA/CoSIRA Rural Employment awards, held in different regions each year, is a measure of what is being done with redundant buildings in the countryside. An astonishing variety of enterprises is represented in the list of entrants, and although some of the buildings are not specifically farm buildings (including such agricultural-related buildings as maltings and breweries, agricultural machinery factories, seedstores and many more) a large number were.

The CLA Farm Buildings Awards have been extended to cover conversions (previously the Henley award dealt with this category). In 1987, the biennial competition attracted 118 entries and the Chairman of the organising committee, Mr. Anthony Duckworth-Chad, commented that "farm tourism and light industrial workshops both appear prominently amongst this year's award winners". The criterion for entry is that the conversions must remain within the ownership of the farm or estate – no developers can qualify.

Other wider-reaching environmental and community awards also potentially reward projects involving the reuse or adaptation of farm buildings. The Times/RIBA Community Enterprise Award, The Times/RICS award, Civic Trust awards and commendations are among those which have included agricultural buildings among recent winners.

The Business Expansion Scheme is a valuable source of capital for small ventures, without the burden of loans or overdrafts, although it does require an initial small injection of capital. The Gretton Report [9] advocated measures to make it more accessible to farmers and landowners setting up new enterprises.

Self help is one way around the difficulties that farmers face. Co-operation between groups of farmers, such as a highly successful exercise in the Framlingham area of Suffolk, which consists of sixty farms, allows the pooling of ideas and resources to good effect. The kind of integrated management plan that is needed, and required by MAFF, to take advantage of the new non-capital grants is far better achieved on this kind of scale and buildings, as much as any other environmental 'feature', should benefit within the overall landscape. Enterprise Trusts for small businesses in the countryside are regularly mooted by the agencies concerned with rural revitalisation, and there must be many ideas and schemes already widely used in the urban context which could be applied to rural problems.

Acres Farm, Bradfield, Berkshire. Beautifully restored, and with the thatch renewed, care has been taken not to spoil the setting with unsightly modern additions. The scheme won a CLA/CoSIRA Rural Employment award in 1986.

PLANNING POLICIES IN ACTION

The last fifteen years have witnessed a gradual sideways shift in the DoE's resolution towards development in the countryside. Until the early 1970s there was a clear presumption against any change of use, outside agriculture, although residential conversion where it seemed the means of preservation was becoming an option. In the later 1970s a stronger emphasis was placed on finding alternative uses for redundant historic buildings whilst their value as a resource, to generate employment, has come to the forefront of the discussion within the last few years.

Whilst the policy notes and changes rain down, it is the local authorities who have to put the theory into practice; checking abuse and excess, encouraging and enabling the well designed and careful schemes into being. Local authorities vary widely in the expertise and professional emphasis of their planning staff. The SAVE report, 'Conservation: A Credit

Account', gives a valuable tally of architectural conservation officers and expenditure, and shows the alarming fluctuation on both, from one part of the country to another.

Situated out there on the battlefront of the argument about the conversion of redundant farm buildings, planning authorities have been learning from mistakes and, in some cases, taking action. Events moved so fast that an initial relative equanimity about residential conversion opened the floodgates, particularly in the Home Counties, East Anglia and much of the south and south west. It became clear that a planning permission for a barn conversion was nothing more, or less, than a licence to build where no other housing development would be permitted – often in the Green Belt. The cynicism with which builders and developers exploited the loophole was matched by the, often, dire architectural results. Usually the 'barn' was sacrificed, in whole or part. The planners had been taken unaware. This has meant that there has been an urgent rethink in many areas of the country, exemplified by the experiences and initiative of Essex County Council who now positively discriminate against residential conversion.

The position in Buckinghamshire illustrates the quandary. As Conservation Officer, Roger Evans, puts it "we pay lip service to the proposition that residential conversion should be the last resort, but in practice it is a fiction". In the Green Belt, where the population is already fairly dense and most barns stand in villages or hamlets, "people object to industrial uses". The best that can be done is to coerce the conversion towards an acceptable standard, easier done with the timber-frame buildings of this area than with the stone barns of the Cotswolds, and to add a condition to planning permission taking away permitted development rights, banning the erection of miscellaneous sheds, walls, fences and "other objects which tend to transform the rural character of barn settings to suburbia. Unfortunately many features which tend to create the latter cannot be controlled". In this case, the County Council enforces any infringements with alacrity.

But, as planners elsewhere pointed out in a recent letter to SAVE, "The question of use is a policy matter on which historic buildings specialist advice is only one consideration . . . much depends on circumstances, location, condition and other aspects of the individual buildings". The fact is that a use compatible with the architectural character of the building may well conflict with other directives concerning the generation of traffic, access and servicing, for instance.

In the National Parks, where a conservation policy might be seen as a higher priority than elsewhere, something of a crisis has arisen. Dartmoor National Park has recently published a review of its policy towards the conversion of redundant traditional buildings within its boundaries. In the section relating to policy, "there will be a presumption for maintaining traditional buildings in their present use and form. Reasonable alterations necessary to adapt farm buildings to modern agricultural use will normally be supported". Nevertheless the conversions steam ahead; applications for conversion to dwellings rose from 22 in 1986/7 to 39 in 1987/8, (taken until January) although those for holiday flats or cottages fell from 29 to 19 in the same period. Many of the developments, in both categories were for three or more units. What is clear from all the figures is that conversion proposals, and completed schemes, are on a continual rise

FIVE VERY LARGE SUSSEX BARNS COMPLETE AND IN SUPERB CONDITION

(Approximately 300 years old)

The careful dismantling of these very large and unique Sussex Barns including outbuildings is due to commence in May. The Barns consist of Sussex Stone, approximately 150,000 Peg Tiles with fittings and a vast selection of prime Oak in all dimensions. Oak of this age, quality and volume will be most suitable for House Building and Renovations, Furniture Manufacturing etc. and can easily be re-assembled back to original Barns.

Serious offers are invited for the purchase either as complete Barns or separate parts thereof. Immediate Inspection of the erect buildings is possible by appointment. For more details please telephone:

DONALD PIKE LTD.
Rushlake Green (043 56) 232 at any time

Other exterior and interior materials will be offered during 1979 from Large Country/Town Houses, Farms, Schools etc. Your enquiries will be noted and dealt with in due course.

FAR LEFT; Church Farm Workshops, Hatley St. George, Cambridgeshire. These nine starter units have been accommodated in a former pig farm.

LEFT; Good Easter, Essex. This barn – part of which dates from the 11th century – is still in farming use but no longer for the storage of the inflammable materials shown in this photograph. Barns like this can be used for storing fertiliser which can be moved with forklift trucks.

THIS PAGE; The nationwide listing resurvey – now nearly complete – should ensure that many barns like this are given statutory protection. However, because of their remote location some will inevitably slip through the net. Equally, many modest farm buildings, whilst important in the landscape and with potential for alternative use, will not merit listing, and will continue to fall prey to dealers in old oak and other materials.

Elkstone, Gloucestershire. Permission has been granted to convert this barn and develop the surrounding land with houses, changing the character of the area from rural to suburban.

despite any hopes to the contrary that the National Park authority might harbour.

In areas where the economic pressures towards residential conversion are becoming hard to resist, the planning authorities have begun to argue the case for alternative uses or, where feasible in the case of a group of farm buildings, to propose a compromise solution. However the difficulties are illustrated by the experience of the South Oxfordshire District Council, fighting plans for residential conversion on a complex of six Grade II, early 19th century listed barns at Fifield Manor Farm, Benson. In August 1987 an appeal against the local authority's refusal of an application for conversion into seventeen dwellings was discussed on the grounds that the scheme would introduce a "seriously incongruous scale" and lead to a "multiplicity of relatively small compartments".

However, the Inspector gave little support to the Council's preference for light industrial use, suggesting that the rentals would be too low to justify an investment of any scale on the buildings and in addition that the roads in the area would not be able to sustain the increase in traffic. Yet the Inspector's report did not touch or offer guidance on the availability of a wide range of grants which might be applied for under light industrial use. Local opinion was also firmly opposed to this type of use, fearful of traffic and, presumably, expansion; yet residential conversion on the scale mooted, at two vehicles per household, would have generated considerable constant traffic in its own right. The current position is that the Conservation Officer, Dr. Malcolm Airs, is arguing for the repair of the major barn, which would remain undivided and in use for casual storage purposes, whilst one barn would be sacrificed for residential conversion. This is a compromise, but a far better outcome than the previous scheme. This approach is similar to the ideas being mooted for the Great Barn at Waxham, Norfolk. Yet as this goes to press, the owners have just applied for listed building consent to demolish. Waxham is listed Grade I. A third example of this thinking, followed the successful outcome of a public inquiry into the residential conversion of a group of farm buildings designed by Sir Edwin Lutyens, at Marsh Court, in Hampshire. This has led to the retention of the main Lutyens barn, which incorporates a granary supported on saddle stones, without alteration and the conversion of adjacent cattle sheds in its stead.

Several County Councils, among them Hampshire and Essex, have produced useful and informative publications surveying the historic farm buildings in their areas and, from that local understanding, putting forward constructive suggestions for their use. Essex County Council's commitment to the cause of historic barns has seen its architects' department carrying out the work on Grange Barn, Coggeshall and, more recently still, the purchase

FAR LEFT, ABOVE AND BELOW; Elkstone, Gloucestershire. Developments like this represent a poor compromise – the building is saved but the setting destroyed. Pressure for new houses in the countryside exacerbates this problem.

LEFT; Furzehall Farm, Fareham, Hampshire. An open-plan office keeps the integrity of this aisled barn. Office and workshop use are, on the whole, less destructive of historic character than residential conversion.

of the splendid Wheat and Barley Barns at Cressing Temple – all three buildings of exceptional importance, and very early date.

Another idea being pursued by Essex County Council has been the idea of 'Rural Town Schemes'. The idea is to borrow the funding pattern of the highly successful Town Scheme, in which the grant costs are shared, 50% by the DoE and 25% by the county and district authorities. At the moment an area on the Essex side of the Stour Valley is being considered as a pilot scheme – particularly suitable because it is an area of special landscape value with scattered farmsteads and hamlets and therefore no existing Conservation Area protection afforded to unlisted buildings. English Heritage could be persuaded into playing their part if the District (Braintree) and the County were seen to be willing to put in their financial contributions. It would probably be a small sum, in tens not hundreds of thousands, but would serve as an important model if others should chose to follow it. This is much along the lines of the idea put forward in the Montagu Report, endorsed by the National Trust and many others, to designate a kind of rural Conservation Area offering the same degree of protection and the same access to grant aid as its urban counterpart. A Rural Conservation Area is also being proposed in Swaledale and Arkengarthdale in the Yorkshire Dales National Park. The purpose is to protect the landscape of stone walls and field barns which are so very characteristic of the area.

Farm buildings which are listed as of

THIS PAGE; Fyfield Manor Farm, Benson, Oxfordshire. This complex of six Grade II listed early 19th century barns was the subject of a public inquiry last year into the refusal of permission for conversion to 17 dwellings. South Oxfordshire District Council considered the scheme to be incongruous. Sadly, the Inspector gave little support to the Council's preference for light industrial use. A revised scheme, keeping the major barn undivided, but sacrificing others for residential use is now under discussion.
OPPOSITE PAGE; The Stables, Colby Estate, near Tenby, Dyfed, Wales. These modest buildings have been converted to provide a basecamp for the National Trust's MSC workforce.

being of architectural or historical interest are, in principle offered automatic protection. However, despite a countrywide relisting scattered rural areas often present a random coverage, and it can never be safely assumed either that an unlisted barn or agricultural building is unworthy, or that a fine building has necessarily been listed. Structure and local plans may be threatened under government thinking, but emphasis is to be placed on more effective strategic planning by District Councils – which are sometimes fit and sometimes unfit bodies to decide on matters of specialist or historic importance. A more flexible instrument of guidance is the non-statutory local plan, on a topic such as the re-use of redundant buildings. These can be prepared more quickly than statutory plans and, where they accord with government policy, will carry weight at appeals. Many existing statutory plans are out of date and this is one way of arguing for shifts of approach.

There has also been a welter of 'design guide' type pamphlets from district councils offering advice on detail and design, emphasising the regional differences and traditional features and in most cases restating the case against residential conversion. Canterbury District Council actually declared a year's moratorium on residential conversions. There are signs that, as their predecessors the residential design guides became blueprints for planning permission, so these are being regarded as a quick way to satisfy the planners – rather than rough guides to practice and approach. Buckinghamshire County Council has never produced a document of this nature; "... no detailed policies on guidance leaflets have been issued at County level. In some ways I think this is a good thing, since despite the provisos explaining that residential conversion is a last resort, leaflets suggesting detailed methods of carrying it out tend to encourage it." (R. Evans, letter to SAVE).

In a wide-ranging report such as this, it is easy to overlook the increasing gulf in planning goals and pressures between different parts of the country. This was brought forcibly home by the Surrey County Planning Officer's comments to SAVE on the situation in his affluent county "We are very conscious of the Government's calls for the generation of jobs in rural areas and for the diversification of agricultural enterprises in the face of falling farm incomes and EEC controls on output. However we have been pressing Government very hard to recognise that such developments, which may be desirable nationally, are in the South East likely to lead to increased urbanisation of the countryside rather than countryside revitalisation". More important still, he continues, "In Surrey, as in much of the South East, neither the unemployment rate nor the general condition of farm buildings justify major departures from existing strict policies aimed at keeping insatiable urban influences out of the Green Belt".

It also must be borne in mind that many of the applicants for planning permission to convert barns and farm buildings are not farmers at all. Many farmhouses have been sold off over the years with an outbuilding or two, and it is often these extra buildings which suddenly appear attractive development propositions in an upwardly spiralling property market. Equally, farmers may have been persuaded to sell off redundant farm buildings for a relatively low sum, which then appear on the market with outline permission for development, with a greatly enhanced value. There are many fast-footed builders and developers exploiting the loopholes in protective planning legislation that the redundant farmstead seems to offer. Planners have been slow on the uptake and with precedents established have to fight their corner that much harder.

Planners have to consider the future as well as the present, when granting consents. If a small business or craft workshop complex should fail the future for the building goes back into the balance and the original intention, to safeguard it, is placed in doubt. Permitted change of use may lead to the provision of costly services, increase of traffic and the setting of a precedent, which may on a further change, lead to less acceptable developments which are, by then, harder to control.

The shift towards deregulation in planning policy by the DoE, as set out in the White Paper, 'Lifting the Burden' (1985) worries those who want to see high standards maintained in the treatment of historic buildings. Another negative development following the early relaxation of planning policy (Circular 22/80) and which it was hoped would en-

LEOMINSTER DISTRICT COUNCIL

■ = TOTAL APPLICATIONS FOR ALL CONVERSIONS

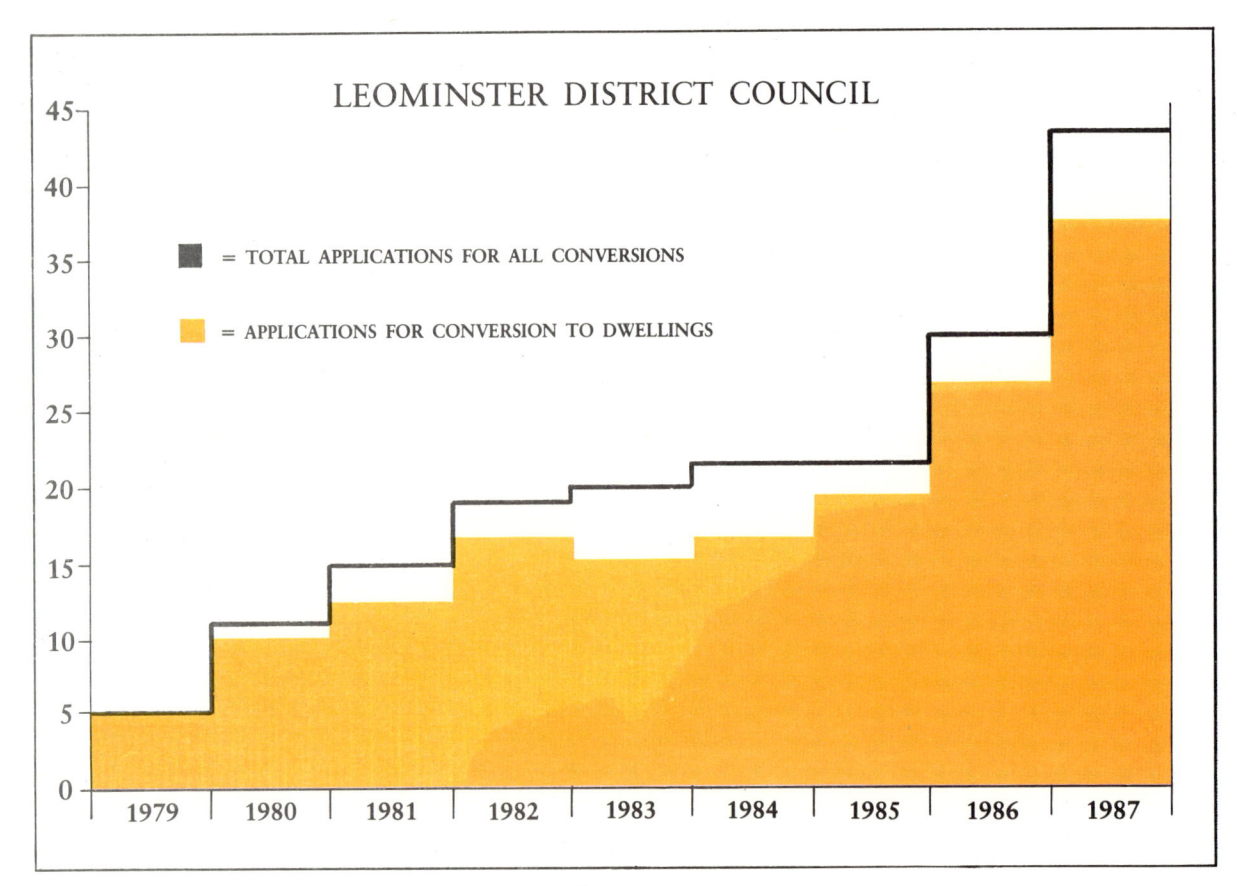

▌ = APPLICATIONS FOR CONVERSION TO DWELLINGS

Hereford and Worcester County Council is one of the few counties to keep computerised records of planning applications and to analyse them. This graph shows the rapid rise in applications for barn conversions in just one rural district, namely Leominster.

As is all too apparent, the overwhelming majority of applications are for residential use (other uses such as office, workshop, etc. form the remainder). The County's records analysis lists numbers of applications rather than numbers of individual units and as large barns and ranges of farm buildings are frequently converted into several units so that the true figure is very much higher.

ABOVE RIGHT; A typical example of a simple stone barn subjected to suburbanisation.

courage the sympathetic reuse of farm buildings, has been the conversion of undistinguished sheds, whilst the historic or architecturally distinguished examples seem not to have gained much by the measures. The result, in the words of one Cambridgeshire planner, has been "a definite own goal".

There has been an alarming rise in the number of successful appeals to the extent that it has become encouraging enough for would-be developers to keep challenging any negative planning decisions. For instance, ten recent South Cambridgeshire refusals of residential conversion were followed by later consents, and a further six allowed on appeal. Not infrequently the eventual conversion leads to the building being de-listed. In Kent, between 1980-86 a total of 1,300 planning applications for change of use of redundant farm buildings were granted consent. Some 624 were refused and of 154 appeals, 47 were allowed. It is fair to assume, given the government's views on the matter, that many more appeals will have been allowed since those figures were presented, overturning the considered views of the district council and denting their authority in these matters. Hereford and Worcester County Council have computerised their records and the table (see p. 40) illustrates the growth in applications across an area of England which comprises both remote rural districts and those directly affected by the Midlands conurbations to their east.

Other threats to the protection offered by the existing planning legislation concern proposals to abolish Structural and Local Plans, the changes to the Use Classes Order and the General Development Order are all bringing, or signalling, relaxations which may not be beneficial. The most recent policy note encouraging the reuse or adaptation of existing buildings is Planning Policy Guidance Note 7: Rural Enterprise and Development, published January 1988. With the circular which weakened the protection to agricultural land, (DoE Circular 16/87) another area of worry opened up, together with threats to the strong controls on development in the Green Belt. Yet the wind seems to blow both ways. Circular 16/87 states a planning principle that the countryside should be protected "for its own sake rather than for the productive value of the land". There one can see evidence of MAFF and DoE compliance, in theory at least. There are some encouraging smoke signals but the major problem remains that of uncertainty; to be effective Green Belt policy and land management policies in general require continuity and firm purpose, both at present sorely lacking. All such vacillation promises ill for historic farm buildings throughout the country.

KENT — Laddingford
Main line station 3 miles. London 36 miles.

Imaginatively converted period barn of outstanding quality

Hall, cloakroom, spacious drawing room with dining and galleries, split level studio/sitting room, kitchen, utility room, 5 bedrooms, luxury bathroom.

Gas central heating.
Period outbuildings.
Landscaped gardens.

Offers in the region of £190,000 freehold

Apply: Tunbridge Wells Office. Tel. (0892) 30176

WEST HENDRED, NR. WANTAGE
M4 10 miles. Oxford 12 miles.
Didcot 5 miles (Paddington 40 minutes).

A SUBSTANTIAL BARN CONVERSION
Vale of White Horse at foot of Berkshire Downs

2 reception rooms, 5 bedrooms, 2 bathrooms. Central heating. Granary (library/study). 2 barns (studio/gallery/conservatory/garage). Delightful gardens about ½ ACRE

GUIDE £150,000

Wantage Office. Tel. Wantage (02357) 4642

SOUTH HAMPSHIRE
Winchester 4¾ miles. Southampton 8 miles.

A MAGNIFICENTLY CONVERTED BARN
with waterside garden and land...

LARGE CONVERTED STONE THATCHED BARN c. 1...
by 25 ft., 2nd stone thatched barn with planning perm...
OFFERS IN THE REGION...

HAMPSHIRE, NEAR WINCHESTER

LATE 18th CENTURY BARN SET IN ABOUT 9 ACRES

...h planning permission for conversion to a single dwelling.

Gloucestershire
Cirencester 4 miles. Tetbury 7½ miles.

A magnifice...
Cotswold st...
delightful a...
setting

3 reception roo...
2 bathrooms, c...
kitchen/breakfas...

Gas central heat...

Double glazing...
superb specificat...
some Elm flooring...

Garaging.
Garden.

Offers in the region...
£175,000 Freehold

Details:
R. A. Bennett & Partne...
Cirencester Office.
Tel. (0285) 5033 or
Humberts, Tetbury Of...
Tel. (0666) 52284

HIGH HALDEN
London 58 miles. Tenterden 3 miles.

...LY CONVERTED PERIOD BARN
...llage. Wealth of exposed oak etc.

Passfield, Hampshire

Price guide: Upon enquiry

Unique country house, skillfully converted from a large 18th century barn, with elevations of stone under a Norfolk reed thatched roof.
Exposed timbers and vaulted ceilings.

Hall. Cloakroom. 3 Reception rooms. Games room.
Fitted kitchen/breakfast room with gas fired Aga.
Utility room. Gas C.H. Minstrels gallery.
5 Bedrooms. Dressing room. 2 Bathrooms.
Garages and stables. Grounds approx 4 acres.

Messenger May Baverstock, 10 The Square, Liphook, Hants.
Tel: (0428) 722031

Stone tent, Chatsworth Estate, Derbyshire. By providing overnight stops for walkers, the stone tent scheme can improve the tourist potential of remote rural areas without any detriment to the landscape. Similar schemes could be initiated in many other regions and, for instance, along long-distance footpaths.

EMPLOYMENT INITIATIVES

The 1980s have seen the emphasis fall increasingly upon employment-generating activities. In the countryside the inexorable fall in agricultural employment, running at 1.5% a year now, has given a different pattern to the crisis, compared to that induced by the fall in manufacturing industry and other labour intensive industries.

Post-war trends to intensification, amalgamation, capitalisation and specialisation in agriculture have, it is now recognised, divorced the industry from the wider rural economy and sometimes led to conflict with other countryside interests. In the uplands, despite support from the EEC through the Less Favoured Areas Directive, rural depopulation and a decline in services have removed the infrastructure upon which the remaining farming community depends. Integrated rural development (IRD) programmes, an initiative sponsored by the EEC, have shown that public authorities can work together effectively to ensure economic, environmental and social interests can be complementary.

The Farm and Countryside Initiatives (F & CI) has been set up as a specifically rural version of the Community Programme of the Manpower Services Commission – to help the long-term unemployed. It aims to link the interested parties with the appropriate agencies or grant or sponsor-giving bodies. Job creation directly linked to building work on the repair of farm buildings is another connection between employment policies and the future for historic farm buildings. The massive reconstruction of Grange Barn, Coggeshall in Essex was carried out as an MSC scheme and following the devastating hurricane which hit the south east and East Anglia in October 1987, there are various proposals to involve county Community Programmes in the urgent business of repairing the damaged structures. Kent has already earmarked projects and has preparations well under way.

The Rural Development Commission is now handling a grants scheme funded by the Department of Employment whilst the Department of Trade and Industry is also a potential source of funds and advice for rural enterprises.

Many flourishing industries began in converted buildings, and then expanded elsewhere. Nor is it anything particularly new. The Historic Farm Buildings Newsletter, January 1988, points out that an Essex jam manufacturers, Wilkins of Tiptree, began in a traditional, and redundant corn barn in 1885. Mr. Wilkin's barn was the setting for a family jam and marmalade-making firm which continues successfully to this day, still at Tiptree.

TOURISM AND LEISURE

Another area which planning authorities are encouraged to view kindly, is that of tourism. Farm diversification in this direction, from farmhouse bed and breakfast to more direct tourist provision opens up the possibility of grant aid under various headings.

Both MAFF and Rural Development Commission grant aid have been recently redirected towards this kind of alternative, farm-based enterprise. Yet there are signs that the conversion of farm buildings to holiday accommodation, even in the prime tourist areas, is running up against a problem of demand, which is enormous but not infinite. West country estate agents, Fox & Sons painted the picture thus, "not surprisingly in a part of the country which attracts such a large number of tourists and holiday makers the first thought everyone has is to create self-catering holiday cottages. Some are good, some are pretty awful, and there is now a concern that, for all the encouragement that has in the past been given... saturation point may be approaching".

Farmers who enter this market will have to be imaginative. In the Peak District National Park one estate agent (quoted in *The Independent*, 3.10.87) had witnessed a virtual revolution, "In the last 18 months I've come across six or seven projects which involve converting farm buildings into riding schools or walking centres". With half the population of England living within sixty miles of the Peak Park the demand is probably there.

Although farmhouse bed and breakfast has long been a British farmer's (and especially, farmer's wife) sideline, France is much further advanced in its links between tourism and farming. In Normandy, a large number of farms sell their produce direct to the public; cheese, cider, calvados are examples. This is promoted by a wide variety of specially marked routes, both scenic and specialist (the *route des fromages* in the Pays d'Auge is one of the latter), and generally confined to back roads. In Britain, farms which lie on the route to major attractions or holiday destinations are the fortunate ones. Many miss out because they do not and an area such as the Lincolnshire Wolds, geographically out on a limb, is unlikely to benefit from tourist-linked farm diversification.

The regional and national Tourist Boards also help finance conversion projects as part of their strategy to promote the development of a less concentrated tourist industry; greater availability in a wider area will spread the burden. In Rural Development Areas, grants are available for employment-creating projects involving tourism and leisure.

Recreational facilities in converted buildings are suitable candidates for grant aid from both the Countryside Commission and the Sports Council. The latter also offers loans, to a maximum of £10,000. Private initiatives, such as swimming pools in converted barns, have shown the way for both public and private sector involvement; Sports Council grants are available for voluntary, statutory and commercial organisations.

The idea of field barns converted into overnight stops for walkers has become a successful one, with room for great potential growth which the Countryside Commission is pursuing in league with the Youth Hostels Association. However, one pioneer in this was the Chatsworth Estate and in their comments to the author of the Reading Report, they cited the two advantages of finding alternative uses for redundant farm buildings; the intangible benefit, which maintains or attains a high amenity value, a landscape which is obviously 'cared for' and the tangible benefit, the income which replaces the loss of traditional farm income.

Pick your own schemes and farm shops are growing fast in southern England, and these, as well as specialist processing businesses are proliferating to supply an increasingly discerning buying public, alert to nutritional factors and sophisticated in their eating habits, but also easily impressed by an image of tradition – as conveyed by the farm-made, cottage-scale surroundings.

Although the countryside and the visiting public can only support a finite number of museums, there has been an astonishing growth including museums of agriculture, those housed in farm buildings, as well as farms run as demonstration projects, either for the methods of traditional agriculture or to show and breed from rare breeds. The Historic Farm Buildings Group in their January 1988 Newsletter added a further thirty-six sites where farm buildings are accessible to the public to an existing list counting eighty-two sites compiled in the Historic Farm Building Study, Sources of Information, produced by the farm buildings group of MAFF in 1986. The full list may well be much longer.

Erw Cerrig Farm, Pandy, Glyn Ceiriog, Clwyd. Both regional and national tourist boards have helped finance conversion projects such as the conversion of barns for holiday conversion as part of their strategy to promote the development of a less concentrated tourist industry.

PART III
DESIGN, CONSTRAINTS AND OPPORTUNITIES

The conversion of historic farm buildings is guided by, on the one hand, the exigencies of the original structure and materials, and on the other, the requirements and adaptations needed for an altered use. If the two aims can be as closely matched as is feasible, so much the better.

If the building is listed, and many more are since the countrywide resurvey, then the planning authority has some leverage in the matter. Many feel that domestic conversion is better confined to unlisted farm buildings (which, of course, still does not rule out the possibility of an outstanding, but unknown, structure being wrecked). This allows the maximum effort to be put into finding an alternative use, more sympathetic to the building, for the listed buildings. In many cases, there is no doubt, adaptive use is the only future for those historic and architecturally distinguished farm buildings that are given a measure of protection under the listing procedures.

When considering how apt a barn or farm building is for conversion, the size of the building will obviously be a major factor. A great threshing barn, many bays long, may be sufficiently spacious to actually contain a separate building within it. Thus a farm shop or office, housed in a portakabin type structure, may be lodged inside requiring absolutely no structural change to the 'host' barn.

Some constraints are offered by the particular type of barn. For example, the aisled barn, with low eaves, "are particularly unsuited to residential use" according to the Cambridgeshire County planners. Orientation is another important determinant; a barn with a south facing private side is much the best option for residential conversion. It means that the more public side, often that along the road, will be the north, and can be left relatively unaltered.

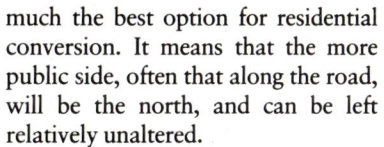

Obviously the choice of use will be guided by realities. Those include the possibility of outside financial aid and the feasibility of gaining planning permission. Another central consideration is location. The remote barn, far from services and the existing infrastructure, is unsuitable for residential use and very probably for light industrial uses either. If permission is granted, the costs which fall upon the owner for installing power and water supplies can be very steep.

Often the kind of employment generating use that most perfectly suits a

OPPOSITE PAGE, FAR LEFT; The variety of local building materials is exemplified by Devon cob.
LEFT; Barn, Fisher's Pond, Eastleigh, Hampshire. This domestic conversion has been commended by the CLA. Its open plan design is sympathetic to the building.
THIS PAGE, ABOVE LEFT; The exterior of Fisher's Pond Barn. The design and location of windows is always the most difficult aspect of a residential conversion.
ABOVE; Interior of a Hampshire chalk barn converted into a house – note the retention of original features. These two conversions were designed by architects Stevenson & Thomas.
LEFT; A very carefully designed barn conversion near Hereford. No changes have been made to the exterior or gable end which are visible from the street.

The picture at the top of this page, taken around 1980, shows a fine stone barn with its stone-tiled roof in a sorry state after years of neglect. A building in this condition is very vulnerable to heavy-handed conversion. This barn was listed Grade II and in order to preserve it a new use needed to be found.

Below is the same building after conversion. To all intents and purposes, the conversion is a reconstruction carried out with little sensitivity or skill – the building boasts a completely new roof with straight ridge line. The courtyard side with its five dormers and protruding porch is no longer recognisable as a barn. This combined with the tarmaced area in front of the new house completely eradicates the building's original rural character.

Former barn at Griggs Farmhouse, Bulmer, Essex. The ridge line here has not been straightened but in other respects this conversion has wrecked the original barn and turned its surroundings into a painfully unsuitable garden. It was recently de-listed.

redundant farm building, is judged by planners to be unsuitable because it will cause and attract traffic on unsuitable roads. Possibly with the current emphasis on employment at all costs, such objections can be more easily countered. Nor is it easy to solve the problem of a single redundant building on a working farm, or when the privacy of the farmhouse is impaired.

If the barn is listed, grant aid based upon the quality of the building is one possibility. It also means that any conversion will have to be carried out with particular care for the structure – exterior and interior. There are enough examples of converted barns (inevitably to residential use) which have been 'de-listed' to show that the system does not prove to be as thorough as one might hope.

There will, in all probability, be some compromises made. The preservation of an historic structure must concentrate on the architectural integrity of the building and retention of its features. In many cases it is enough that the external character should survive the transformation relatively unaltered, in others (particularly fine timber framed structures) the interior is no less important.

Some planning authorities are very pessimistic about what they are seeing. In Cornwall for example "The County Council's policy, through its

RIGHT; Slate hung granary, Cornwall. This modest but characterful building has been discreetly converted into an office.

FAR RIGHT; A barn in a village centre, Leicestershire, crudely converted to a house. It has both dormer and Velux windows piercing the roof and the design of other windows and openings is wholly out of sympathy, both in materials and detailing.

Structure Plan and Countryside Local Plan is to encourage the conversion of redundant buildings in the countryside provided that they make a significant visual contribution and that the conversion retains the existing character of the building . . . the second criterion is seldom fulfilled. I appreciate that one does not necessarily want to see a lot of derelict old buildings in the countryside but, quite frankly, the way in which farm buildings are being 'saved' leads one to wonder whether that would not be preferable" (recent letter to SAVE).

Specifically on domestic conversions the picture is grim. The letter continues. "With a notable exception of the National Trust, clients do not seem to have the wish and/or their designers the ability to treat these buildings sensitively. Even in the few instances in Cornwall where they have been treated well, the 'infrastructure' of present day living, garages, parking spaces, aerials, washing lines, etc., greatly diminish any reasonable effect which may have been achieved". Planning officers around the country echo this view. The accoutrements of domestic life do not sit well with the simple, functionalism of barns or farm buildings.

Yet it must be said that planners have themselves to blame. In many areas all advice given is directed towards domestic conversion – albeit to improve the standard of design. The outcome is that these documents become, by default, a sort of 'design guide' with, obviously enough, the applicant feeling reassured of a planning permission the closer the scheme remains to the suggested principles in the local authority leaflet.

By contrast, this simple conversion of a barn at Elkstone, Gloucestershire, shows an understanding of regional style and no attempt has been made to obliterate all signs of its original purpose.

CONTROLS

Although there are nominal checks on the flaunting of planning controls in the conversion of listed buildings, they are unfortunately all too rarely exercised. Planning authorities in Buckinghamshire recently took action successfully to prosecute for works carried out not in accordance with consent at Cuddington, and in another case threatened action until the works were remedied. De-listing is another, *post hoc*, punitive measure which stops the building in question being suitable for grant aid. Whether the ignominy of a de-listing affects a careless converter is open to question. In Buckinghamshire, five farm buildings have been de-listed within one district (Wycombe). In Cambridgeshire, another county under pressure, "at least eight listed barns converted to residential after re-survey are no longer listable (one completely demolished)" commented Conservation Officer, John Preston.

The relaxation of the Building Regulations (1985) has been a great boon to the conversion of historic buildings. The Reading Report summarised the main changes which would benefit converted buildings. Past usage and experience are now allowed as a method of justifying the use of traditional materials and workmanship. Minimum requirement in the heights of habitable rooms have been dispensed with. Zones of space serving windows to habitable rooms have also been dispensed with. Enshrining expectations which were highly unrealistic in the case of many historic buildings, the regulations were often the cause of delay, unsatisfactory design and even the defeat of a scheme.

ESSEX COUNTY COUNCIL

OPPOSITE PAGE, ABOVE LEFT; A former barn at Taynton, Oxfordshire, shows a confused elevational treatment.
ABOVE RIGHT; Town Farm Barn, Hatfield Broad Oak, Essex. A nasty outbreak of Velux windows dominates the roof of this 14th century listed barn. These together with standard doors and windows, give little clue to its antiquity.
BELOW LEFT; Farm complex at Bangor on Dee, Clwyd. One barn has already been converted and the range to the left is the next in line for unsympathetic treatment. Poor window detailing yet again lets this scheme down.
BELOW RIGHT; Barn at Rippingales, Belchamp Walter, Essex. There is little to suggest this is an historic farm building. Indeed, since conversion, it has been delisted.
THIS PAGE, FAR LEFT; Sonning, Berkshire. A barn which, though retaining its thatch, has been mutilated with bland windows and an unfortunate link building.
LEFT; Barn conversion, Great Leighs, Essex. This is an attempt – which conspicuously fails – to give interest to the new fenestration of a barn. Again, any sense of the building's original character has been dissipated.

QUALITY

Once a building has been earmarked for conversion, its future potential use and the finance settled, the worries are by no means over. The 1987 Countryside Caretakers Award, sponsored by the Countryside Commission and the Royal Welsh Agricultural Society, was awarded that year for 'sensitive conversion of traditional farm buildings of importance in the landscape' and 'focussed specifically on the quality of design and craftsmanship of the conversion as the prime criterion for selection'. The judges comments tell the sad story, "... all entries were let down by design and use of insensitive materials such as plastic guttering and windows, pebble dash, asbestos slate and badly designed skylights. In part this was the result of cost constraints but the judges felt that more thought could have been given to using traditional materials which are not necessarily more expensive over the lifetime of a building. If care is not given to this there is danger that the majority of surviving traditional farm buildings will be either changed out of all recognition or derelict in ten years time".

PUBLICITY AND INFORMATION

Information and guidance are crucial where the conversion of farm buildings is concerned. How that guidance should be given is a matter for each local authority. Cambridgeshire, for example, put together a mobile illustrated exhibition entitled "Barn Conversions: Answers or Problem?" This toured local libraries during 1987. Other local authorities would do well to follow this example.

But the fact remains that for most farmers, now as ever, the knotty problem of finding a use, grant aid and submitting for planning permission is far beyond their experience or expertise. Invariably, if they are thinking along these lines, the first port of call will be the ministry, probably in the shape of their local ADAS office. It is only those with more than average persistence and initiative who will find their way to the myriad other sources of advice, and quite possibly, finance. Much of the problem for a reuse for farm buildings is an information problem. How many farmers know about the Sports Council grant aid, for example; according to the Sports Council, no such applications for the conversion of farm buildings have been received. Yet private ventures into inserting swimming pools, for example, into barns show that this is a successful idea which goes far towards the ideal of not impinging on the fabric of the building.

For surviving traditional farm buildings, information on maintenance has been sadly unforthcoming from MAFF. A useful leaflet, written by architect John Sell for the SPAB, outlines how to carry out 'first aid repairs' – under two headings, problems caused by structural movement and those caused by water penetration. The old adage, 'a stitch in time saves nine' is peculiarly fitting to the problems of aging buildings, where a slipped tile ignored may bring the roof down, and with it the building, whilst a slipped tile replaced will ensure a long, useful life for the structure. Guidance, in an accessible form, may determine the future for a redundant building, while its future is decided.

The best use for an old building is the one for which it was built: many barns can accommodate modern machinery.

USES

The planning authorities' consensus of 'preferred uses' starts with ancillary agricultural uses, community, recreation and tourist facilities, crafts and light industrial uses and place residential use at the bottom of the list. The dilemma is that it is in this latter area that the highest level of investment is available, often involving the most radical alteration to the original fabric and setting.

The number of domestic conversions of barns and whole farmsteads is accelerating. With restrictions on new building in many of the most attractive and well protected areas of the country, a planning permission for an existing building is an open door. It can also, with sufficient neglect to the building, leave a cleared site upon which a new house can rise.

One attraction of conversion to industrial, or employee-generating use, in preference to residential use, is the way in which the financial return is made. In the latter, it comes as a one-off, lump sum, in the other, successfully run, the income will continue to come in, year after year. In the guidance notes produced by the NFU for members considering the conversion or adaptation of a redundant farm building, this point is emphasised. The decision to go for an instant return may well, after all, be a faulty one.

The Reading Report listed the main categories of reuse reported in its survey; after the various residential conversions (including an old person's home), the list included agricultural engineering, kennels, garden centre, maggot-breeding business, public house or club, village community centre, high tec industry, wholesale warehouse, as well as the more obvious craft workshops, farm shops, museums and offices. The message is that farm buildings, provided they offer suitable location, and space can be adapted to almost anything.

LEFT; Farm buildings at Rayson Hall, Townhead, Cumbria, have been converted for a cake-making enterprise, Lakeland Gateaux Ltd. This scheme also won a CLA award.

FAR LEFT, AND BELOW; Hole House, Haltwhistle, Northumberland. This is a good example of a small farm complex which has been carefully converted and provides valuable local employment. The setting of the farm has been preserved. This scheme (grant-aided by the Rural Development Commission) won a CLA award.

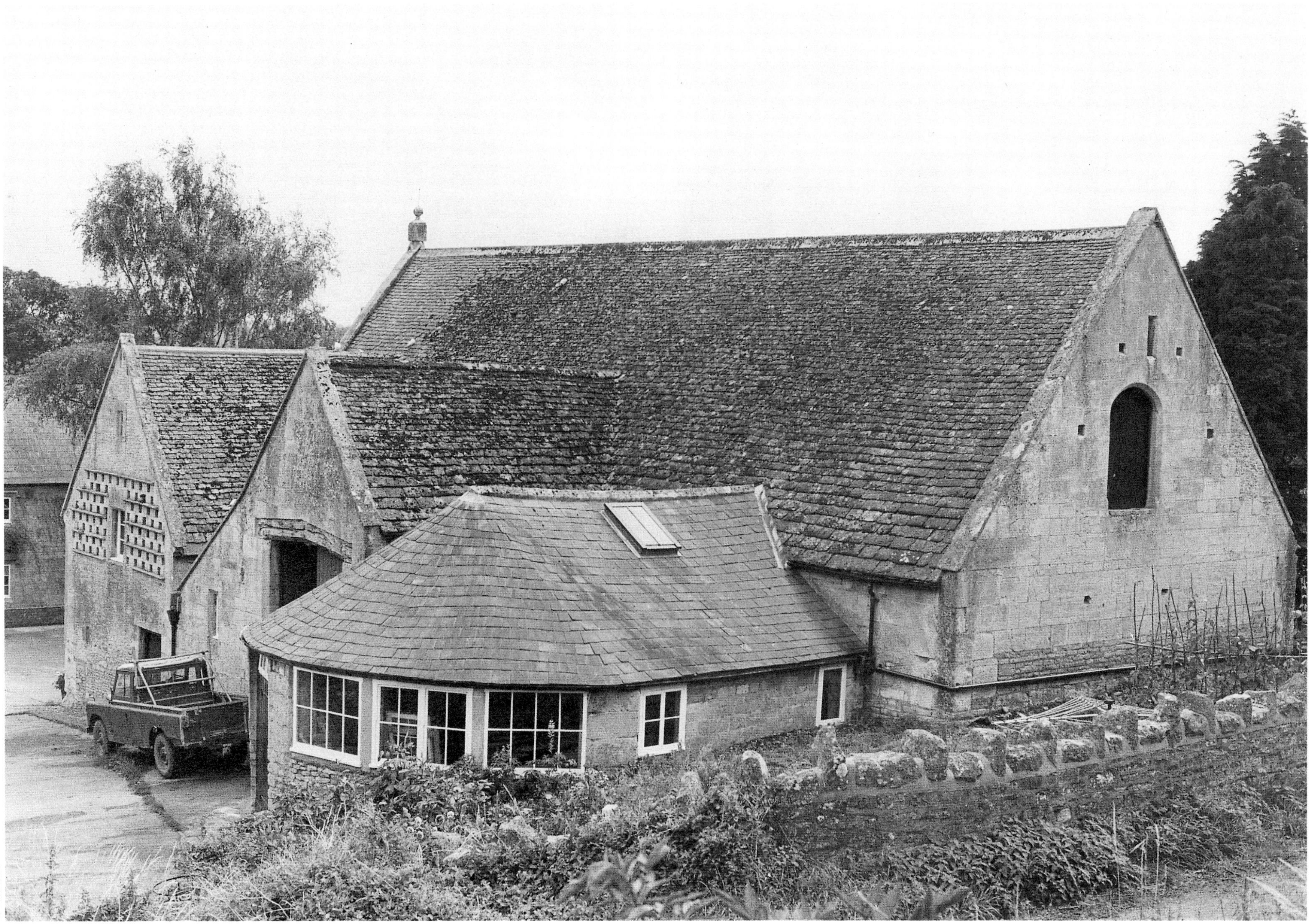

R.C.H.M.E.

DESIGN DETAIL

What is clear from a consensus of the many guidelines drawn up by local authorities, as well as local and national amenity societies, is that a traditional barn is rarely a good choice for a house – unless the occupants are prepared to live in a house of abnormal proportions, and without the usual arrangements of a house, old or new. A Hampshire architect, Huw Thomas, who has carried out a number of barn conversions puts it thus, "For whatever purpose the barn is to be used, what grins through in the end is still a barn; its new function must always be secondary to this". He continues, "Everything I do is about levels and spaces and galleries, so that the cathedral of oak that you see in these barns is heightened".

Lighting the interior of a barn is likely to be the main stumbling point. Off-the-peg windows and a rash of roof lights are two of the principal ways to wreck a fine barn. For Huw Thomas, "The charm of a barn is in the massing of the roof. If I have to put in roof lights I feel that I've failed.... Windows are all-important, and that's where most clients go wrong once they've got their planning and building regulations approvals; they *will* put in standard windows".

The slippage between the planning application and the outcome is a topic that Thomas, with many others, expresses great concern about. In his view, "where listed buildings are concerned, it ought to be a national policy to make building regulations drawings part of the listed building consent.... the planning procedure... allows the client to use an architect to get planning and building regulations approval, but once these have been achieved, to ignore the architect's design and produce an inferior conversion". To circumvent this, requires vigilance on the part of planners, which staffing levels rarely permit. The Weald of Kent Preservation Society introduces its leaflet on barn conversions with a disclaimer on the suitability of historic barns to residential use. But "if a residential conversion it must be, then we feel strongly that local planning authorities should be much stricter about imposing architectural conditions than they have been in the past".

Other solecisms relating to design include the thoughtless subdivision of interior spaces, inappropriate detailing of both interior and exterior, cheap replacement materials for roof or cladding, badly sited insertions of flue and vent pipes, fencing, gardens and extra buildings (sheds, garages, etc.) which do not reflect the scale or nature of the building. These and many other heresies the planning department may well have no control over. Incremental change over the years can worsen the situation.

English Heritage is producing a publication dealing with the design aspects of barn conversions, but it is long overdue and as time passes, so the atrocities that pass for barn conversions mount up.

OPPOSITE PAGE; Medieval barn and dovecote, South Stoke, Avon. This barn is still in agricultural use. The horse engine house is an addition of c.1800. The roofscapes of barns are all important.
LEFT; Former barn, Great Shelford, Cambridgeshire. This could be a new building. The district council refused planning permission for conversion but the applicants won permission on appeal. In this situation, the local authority has very little control over details of design. This building has a new roof and standard windows and is thoroughly unsympathetic.

EXAMPLES: TITHE BARNS

Although tithe barns by their sheer scale present dramatic problems when they fall into disrepair, they also tend to be buildings of sufficient recognised value, architecturally and historically, that raising funds – though arduous and time-consuming – is usually a possibility. The barns mentioned below illustrate many timescales, and in one or two cases, buildings have been brought back from dereliction or partial collapse, as in the case of Coggeshall. These barns are frequently referred to as cathedrals among barns, and we should not be blinded by success stories (however hard won those successes might have been) and forget the hundreds upon hundreds of 'parish churches' among barns where public money is less available and where individual initiative must take the burden of maintaining and using them.

Conversion of the larger structures is often least harmful if the building can be considered as a shell, and a small portakabin type building slotted in, as farm shop, office or similar. Titchfield Abbey in Hampshire, built before 1400, was repaired with funds from the, then, Historic Buildings Council, now English Heritage. Such assistance is offered on the understanding that a building must be made accessible to the public. In this case, where the farmer was instrumental in efforts to save the building, a happy solution was arrived at with the barn being used to house a farm shop, self contained at one end of the immense space. Elsewhere there is abundant space to store pallets and machinery. This means that the requirement to give the public access is fully complied with and the barn is in viable use.

Another large barn, Church Barn, Edlestone in Bedfordshire, has recently been converted to offices. Here galleries have been inserted so that the main space remains clear. The work was carried out under the supervision of the Ancient Monuments arm of English Heritage, (the barn was scheduled in the 1920s) although, surprisingly in the circumstances, the developers did not employ an architect. Fenestration, both in walls and roof, has been added but the structure of the eleven-bay aisled barn is largely intact, with space made available by the insertion of galleries. Previously obscured by a number of massive grain dryers, the structure of the barn is once again largely visible.

So far an unresolved problem,

though not without want of effort, is Waxham Barn in Norfolk which has been a cause for concern for many years. An outstanding 16th century barn, listed Grade I, it is part of a manorial group which includes the Hall, perimeter walls and gatehouse, with the church close by. It was estimated in 1985 when Norfolk County Council produced a valuable report "on its historical importance, present conditions and the options for financing its repair" that repairs would cost £163,000; three years later that figure has soared. Recently it has been the subject of a compulsory purchase order by the County Council following the issuing of a repairs notice with which the owner failed to comply. Now the owner has lodged an appeal and pending the outcome, the Council has carried out emergency repairs at its own expense. A feasibility study has been prepared and future uses for the barn and the low stock-shed wings which flank it, are being considered. One interested potential purchaser would use the barn which is an astonishing 19 bays long, as a store for traditional building materials, but the economics point to the wings being converted to residential use, a conclusion reinforced by the reluctance of English Heritage to consider grant aid unless a viable alternative use outside agriculture could be found. In the County Planner's words, "This has proved to be the sticking point."

Grange Barn, Coggeshall in Essex, was a Cistercian Abbey barn which on the evidence of the joinery techniques, seems to have been completed in the mid 12th century. The story of its rapid decline, in less than twenty years, after eight centuries of continued use and maintenance, is a sorry one. The owner had decided around 1960 that the barn was no longer of agricultural use, but it was not listed (Grade II*) until 1966. The building began to deteriorate rapidly. A local group, the Coggeshall Grange Barn

FAR LEFT; Waxham Barn, Norfolk. This is an exceptional (Grade I listed) building of 16th century date and part of an outstanding group of buildings – yet it has recently been the subject of an application to demolish. The County Council is meanwhile pursuing a compulsory purchase order and emergency repairs are being carried out. Disagreement about the possible future use of the barn has not helped.
LEFT; Waxham Barn: interior. A majestic space, 19 bays long, which could in principle house a wide variety of uses.

Coggeshall Barn, Essex, in 1964. The building was only listed in 1966, after it had begun to decay. After 800 years of agricultural use, it was allowed to fall into disuse and maintenance was neglected. As a consequence, the cost of repairs steadily spiralled and its very survival was thrown into doubt. An independent trust was set up to save the barn and, after protracted legal wrangles, the work was carried out in 1984-85. The restoration was an heroic undertaking, and has produced a building of immense value to the local community.

Trust was formed to fight for its future. In 1973 repair costs had been estimated at £25,000; the result of the following years of inaction was that by the time the work was carried out, in 1984-5, it was to cost £255,000.

After a long series of wrangles, including two public enquiries, Braintree District Council bought the barn on a compulsory purchase order and large grants were made available, over £100,000 from English Heritage and a loan of £42,500 from the Architectural Heritage Fund, with the County Council as guarantor, in July 1984.

Once the importance of the building within the early history of European timber framed buildings had been established, funds became easier to find. Thus there are direct benefits from the efforts of local authorities, as in the case of Waxham (above), to produce a detailed report on a building of outstanding quality. Unfortunately many counties, even rich ones, such as Dorset, who were unable to respond to SAVE's queries on redundant farm buildings in their area, do not have the expertise or the will to do the essential scholarly spade-work. The other crucial ingredient at Coggeshall was the local effort to raise further funds, both from a long list of charitable foundations and trusts, and from local fund-raising activities. A dedicated committee of tireless volunteers is a valuable asset, and ensures local interest and support, in the long-term.

Once apparently derelict beyond rescue, Coggeshall has been restored to very high standards, using riven chestnut laths in the roof so that the

By the 1970s, the barn had fallen into a seemingly desperate state of dereliction and the timber frame was itself in a condition of near collapse. It was clear that a complete restoration was urgently needed. Compulsory purchase and the provision of generous grants saved the great barn.

LEFT; The restoration work was done to a very high standard, using traditional construction methods to preserve its original appearance.

essential characteristic irregularity of the ridge is preserved. Manpower Services Commission labour was a major contributory factor to the rescue and well supervised, the job was carried out immaculately. It is now used for a wide range of community functions.

In autumn 1987 Essex County Council bought the farm at Cressing Temple, on which the famous Wheat and Barley barns stand. In this case, the barns were in excellent shape, having been conscientiously maintained by the farmer and kept in agricultural use of some sort until the sale. The question mark here is to find a suitable use for an enormous floor area.

Cressing Temple barns, Essex. The problem here was not one of decay or neglect – the buildings had been very well maintained, but were no longer of any use for agricultural purposes. The solution in this case was the purchase of the entire farm complex by Essex County Council. The question was that of an appropriate use. The great tithe barns may be the "cathedrals" of vernacular architecture, but this does not mean that their future is always assured. Indeed, as the cases of Coggeshall and Waxham indicate, the finest examples may be threatened with total destruction. The very scale of the buildings, and the inappropriateness of many potential uses, exacerbates the problems.

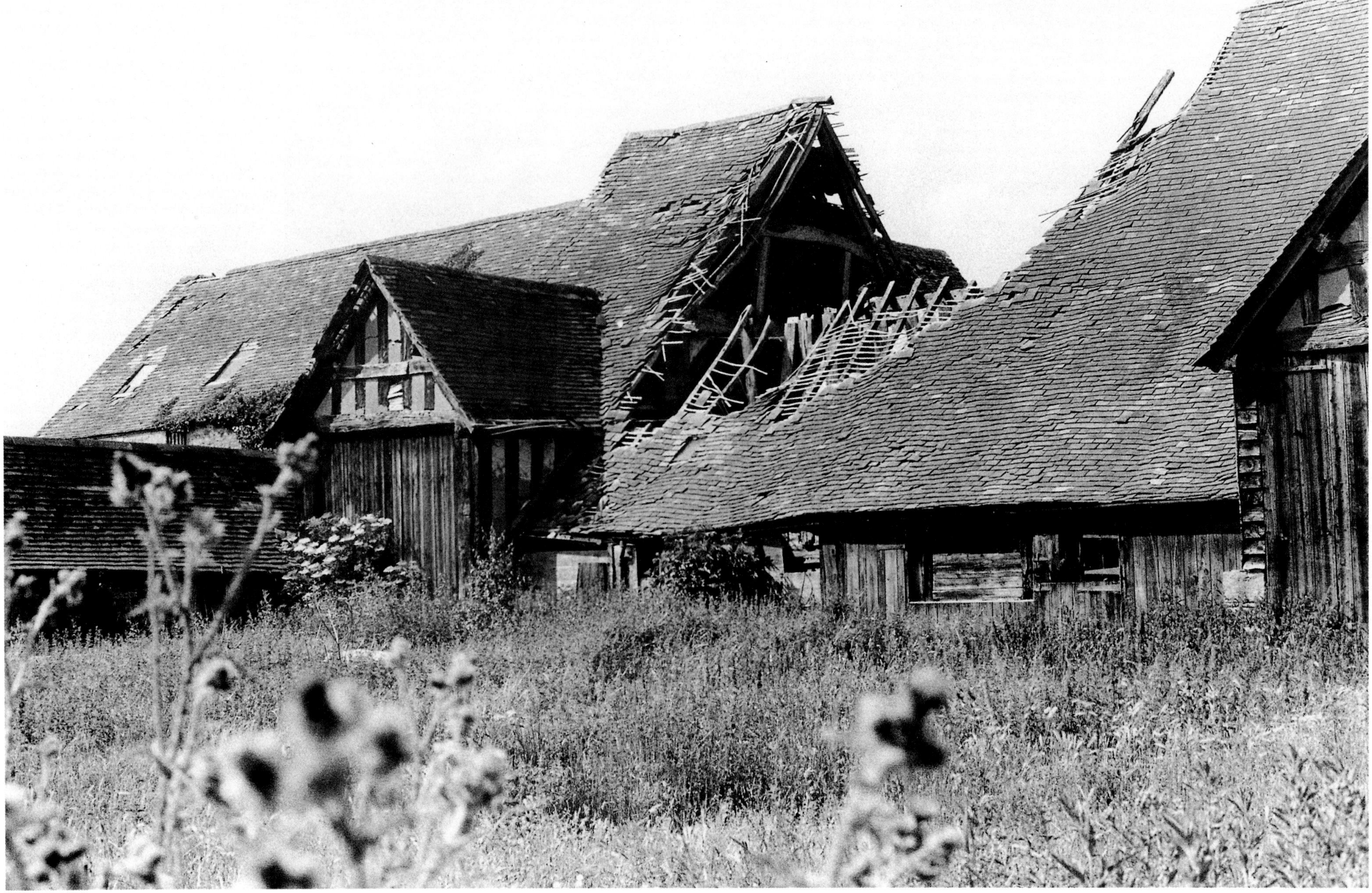

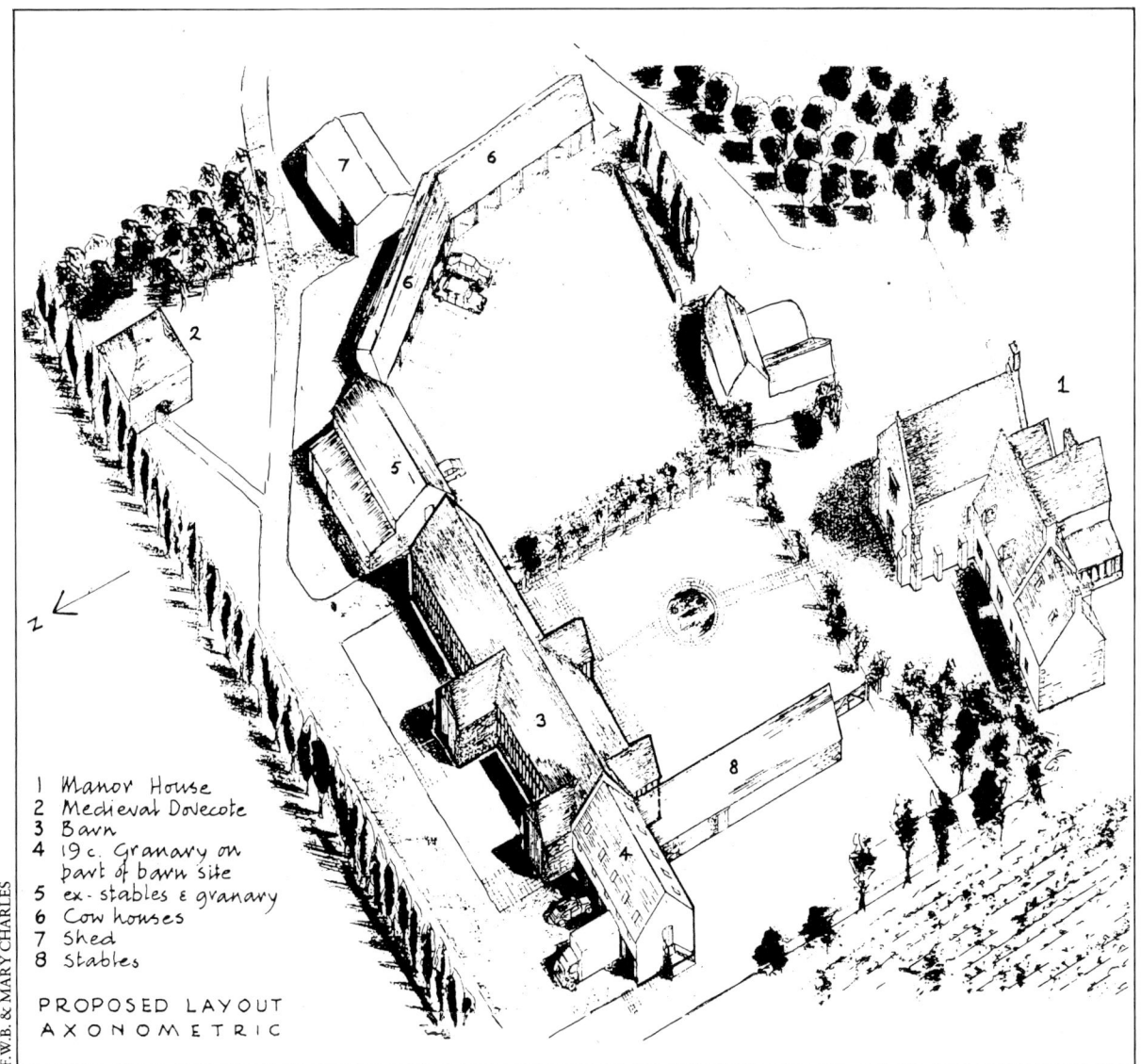

1. Manor House
2. Medieval Dovecote
3. Barn
4. 19c. Granary on part of barn site
5. ex-stables & granary
6. Cow houses
7. Shed
8. Stables

PROPOSED LAYOUT AXONOMETRIC

F.W.B. & MARY CHARLES

Another great barn, Bretforton tithe barn, near Evesham is being converted into a theatre. Its owners, who already have a small theatre to seat around a hundred in the house, Bretforton Grange, plan to double capacity by making use of the barn. At the time of writing the first phase of repairs, stabilising the structure, are under way. The cost of £120,000 is being funded with the help of a 40% English Heritage grant, while £7,000 has been offered by the County Council and District Council. The second phase, for which funds are being actively sought at the moment, will see the barn converted into a theatre, preserving the building without subdivision, and with its spaces left clear. Bretforton had been threatened with conversion into dwellings which would, obviously, have destroyed the integrity of the building as it stands. Architects F W B and Mary Charles have already repaired two outstanding tithe barns in the area, both in the care of the National Trust, Middle Littleton and Bredon, the latter after it was badly damaged in a fire in 1980.

Leigh Court Barn in Worcestershire is to be taken into guardianship by English Heritage, and they have committed themselves to spending £500,000 on urgent repairs. As both a Grade I listed building and a scheduled ancient monument it is offered the

OPPOSITE PAGE; Tithe barn, Bretforton, Worcestershire. This fine barn dates from the second half of the 15th century and was built for the Abbey of Evesham. It is part of a notable farm group at Bretforton. It fell into a sad state of disrepair and this accelerated in recent years. Conversion into housing was proposed but rejected – it would have been utterly destructive of the building's character. Repair work costing £120,000 is now under way. The barn is then to be converted to house a theatre, a use which will leave the interior unobstructed.

LEFT; This axonometric drawing shows the whole historic farm group at Bretforton. This includes buildings of post-medieval date up to the 19th century. Repair work at Bretforton has come none too soon: the principal roof structure was beginning to collapse. But now the roof is being carefully repaired – it is an important example of late medieval carpentry.

Leigh Court Barn, Worcestershire. This barn is of exceptional importance, dating from c. 1300 and built for the monks of Pershore Abbey. It is listed Grade I and is a scheduled Ancient Monument. It is another example of an outstanding barn with no obvious economic use, though its owners were anxious to see it retained. The interior is of great nobility, with a fine 150 ft. run of huge oak crucks supporting the roof. It is the largest cruck building in the country.

highest level of legal protection for a building. The transaction which makes English Heritage responsible for the repair, maintenance and management of the barn still leaves the barn the legal property of the Stewarts, who have farmed Leigh Court for generations. Re-roofing is a priority, but none of the magnificent oak crucks will need replacing. Almost 150 feet long, Leigh Court Barn dates from *c.* 1300 and was a storage barn for Pershore Abbey. After the works have been completed in spring 1989, the barn will be open to the public.

The Great Barn, Gawthorpe is a Lancashire stone aisled barn, dating from the first decade of the 17th century. Its conversion to a multi-purpose hall, for performances, exhibitions and conferences is a partnership between the National Trust, Lancashire County Council, Nelson and Colne College (who manage it for educational purposes) and Manpower Services Commission who provided labour for the project, phased over a number of years from 1980 onwards. Unusually, the barn had already been converted, for Burnley Football Club. Work involved removal of a nine inch thick concrete floor and remaking walls where modern windows had been inserted. The barn is scheduled to open fully this year.

A number of tithe barns are in the care of the National Trust and a further number are scheduled Ancient Monuments. They, in principle, are assured careful maintenance and a future without threat. Many others survive in whole or partial use, by the efforts of farmers and land owners who value them, not regarding them as economic encumbrances but assets, assisted in some cases by the injection of grant aid or support from local authorities or other bodies.

The priority is to know where those that remain vulnerable and English Heritage's Buildings at Risk Register was set up to monitor the size of the problem and to ascertain the number of vulnerable buildings, of which barns and farm buildings are an obvious sizeable percentage. However, nothing has so far come of this beyond a pilot study in a single council area (Kirklees, in Yorkshire) the results of which are not yet available. English Heritage cannot provide even a check list of Grade I listed barns in the country – so far there is no way of getting statistics to even begin to measure the scale of the problem for outstanding buildings in this category. What hope for the lesser ones?

Leigh Court Barn has been used for many purposes, including the making of cider (presses remain). The barn is being taken into guardianship by English Heritage, which will spend £500,000 on repairs. It is planned to open it to the public in spring, 1989.

BARNS, LARGE, MEDIUM AND SMALL

A full sized barn is probably as flexible as any agricultural building. It is likely to be big enough to house large-scale machinery, unless it is aisled, in which case only the central space will be full height. In such cases grain bins can be slotted into the aisle space, whilst full size grain silos are often housed in large barns. Smaller threshing barns are often converted to milking parlours, to storage or processing of produce, or as livestock accommodation, perhaps with temporary subdivisions.

The determinant of what can be done with a barn tends to be its structure. Timber framed barns are not suited by sub-division into small rooms, as a domestic use tends to require, and this leads to the destruction of important structural elements, cutting into main beams and patching up with alien materials. More importantly the quality of a timber framed barn of any quality is in the exposed carpentry, in its sense of scale, space and proportion – all of which are threatened by the usual inflexible residential requirements. Quite simply, the building does not suit the new use.

One problem relating to timber framed barns is the vexed question of moving the structure. The SPAB has always resisted this as a solution but most others concerned with the future of agricultural buildings are prepared to countenance the occasional heresy, if it ensures a future for the building and possibly, proves to be a way of resisting domestic conversion. At the time of writing, Suffolk brewers Greene King are re-erecting the fine barn from Wetherden Hall Farm, Kettlebaston, dating from 1450, as a restaurant to be attached to the Rushbrooke Arms, Sicklesmere, near Bury St. Edmunds. The solution came about because Babergh District Council turned down an application for residential conversion – requiring the building to be accessible to the public. It is proving possible to use 95% of the original timbers, of a building some twenty metres long, while repairs to a damaged gable are being made from old timbers from an extension to the barn, long gone. Some years ago, a barn at Knebworth House was removed a few hundred yards, also to provide a restaurant.

Outside Wantage, five redundant local barns have been reconstructed and form a linked courtyard scheme sited in a chalk quarry. Serving as a Youth Hostel and community centre, it takes its *raison d'être* from being midway along the Ridgeway Long Distance path. It serves local educational needs, offers almost seventy

OPPOSITE PAGE; Wetherden Hall Barn. This splendid 15th century barn, originally at Wetherden Hall Farm, Kettlebaston, Suffolk, has been re-erected as an extension to the Rushbrooke Arms, Sicklesmere, by the brewers, Greene King. Moving buildings of this quality must be a matter of last resort: an historic building is one with its site. But in this case, residential conversion had been rejected by the local authority, which wanted a use with public access. No such use could be found. The interior was remarkably intact, but the barn had been re-roofed in corrugated iron. It is over 60 feet long and in only one section – a partly collapsed gable – had it seriously decayed. Fortunately, a quantity of timber from a demolished extension was available for repairs.

THIS PAGE, ABOVE; Wetherden Hall Barn. Re-erection in progress at Sicklesmere, near Bury St. Edmunds. Some 95% of the original timberwork was re-used. The necessary changes to the building – insulation, heating, lighting and other services – were easily accommodated within the timber frame. The loss of a building's historic context is a serious concern, but in this case it has gained an improved setting and is accessible to the public for the first time. The restoration of the exterior has included the replacement of corrugated iron roofing with clay tiles.

BELOW; Manor Farm, Knebworth House, Hertfordshire. Two fine barns stand in the grounds of Knebworth House. In 1971-72, they were removed to their present locations under the direction of Donald Insall & Associates and converted into restaurants. The Manor Barn was moved in one piece, a technique which is viable in the case of timber-framed buildings.

Court Hill Ridgeway Centre, near Newbury, Berkshire. The Court Hill Centre is a Youth Hostel and community centre, housed in a linked group of five barns, all transplanted from locations in the neighbourhood of Newbury. Accommodation is provided for walkers on the Ridgeway and there are two holiday flats. One of the barns provides a large public space, used as a refectory and for social events. The Centre provides accommodation for up to 70 people – mostly in bunkhouse style accommodation of this kind. New finishes, necessarily economical, have been kept simple and the alterations are in sympathy with the character of the building.

bunk beds to different standards from basic dormitories to the more comfortable heated cabins, and there are two holiday flats and a warden's house in addition. The Court Hill Ridgeway Centre was the initiative of the same man who restored Lains Barn (nearby) as a community centre and conference venue some years ago. Dr. Dick Squires received a *Times/RIBA* Community Enterprise Award in 1987 for his latest venture, which had received sponsorship from local authorities, the Countryside Commission, the regional Tourist Board as well as a number of charitable trusts – proof that funds are available, if an individual or group has the energy and determination to identify them and make a strong enough case to warrant financial backing. As Dr. Squires said of Lains Barn, quoted in the Montagu Report, "On the advantage of using a converted barn for social events: it is unique, individual and an experience, a happening to enter – makes the blood run hot. (I don't get this feeling entering the Civic Hall). Space. Cheap to use".

Compared to the timber framed barns which do allow for dismantling (and a trade in their sale for re-erection which led to a number of cases, and even prosecutions, for the illegal removal of listed buildings) barns constructed from load-bearing stone walls are much more vulnerable to crass external change. The traditional stone barn, almost stark in its simplicity and broken by little more than its big doors and a few ventilation slits, is immediately ruined by fussy fenestration or additions which detract from its scale and simplicity.

Stone and thatch are a marvellous combination of traditional materials and still have their propagandists. Philip Hughes, Technical Secretary of the SPAB received a letter of recommendation from the Dillington Estate Office, referring to the "benefit which old thatched barns have when it comes to storing agricultural produce. We have a very large old thatched barn with doors at one gable end for ease of access for modern tractors and trailers. The insulation benefits of the very thick stone walls . . . and the thatch itself is extremely useful for storing potatoes. Without any use of modern temperature and humidity control methods the potatoes store extremely well over the winter and, furthermore, last well into the early summer before starting to sprout – thus great advantage is taken of the end of season price rise before the early potato market gets under way".

For those who use traditional buildings for storage of perishable fruit or vegetables, another option is the insertion of a coldroom – apple stores in oast houses and a strawberry store in a traditional barn near King's Lynn are examples given by one firm who install such equipment. A coldroom is a totally self-contained unit, which can be plugged into a power supply and be sited either freestanding or wall mounted, where there is a low ceiling height.

There is no shortage of examples around the country of adaptive uses for small barns, particularly classic stone ones, which have not required much alteration at all. A Somerset cider barn has been converted to a smoke-house, specialising in eels, and another highly successful enterprise smoking and processing fish operates from Cotswold barns in Winson, Gloucestershire.

Another category of barn is the field barn, mentioned above. Here the location, out in the fields, and the tiny proportions, have presented a great problem for further use. The solution which has been attempted, and which is being more widely investigated, is that of a basic overnight stopping place, a 'stone tent' or 'bunkhouse barn'. This way there does not need to be large apertures or expensive alterations – the building with a few essential amenities, is fine as it is.

The Countryside Commission has produced a useful report on the conversion of field barns to camping use in the Peak District and concluded that, on the basis of earlier experiment

LEFT; Blake House Farm Barn, Great Saling, Essex. Adaptive re-uses of barns around the country have included a considerable number involving new rural industries. In this case, a barn serves as a workshop for the manufacture and restoration of furniture.

ABOVE; Brightlingsea Hall Barn, Essex. This is another successful Essex conversion. The barn is now a thriving toy factory.

BELOW; Granary, Ipsden, Oxfordshire. Even the most specialised historic farm building types can find a use appropriate to modern agricultural practice. The form of this granary – elevated above the ground and windowless – makes it extremely suitable for use as a pesticide store.

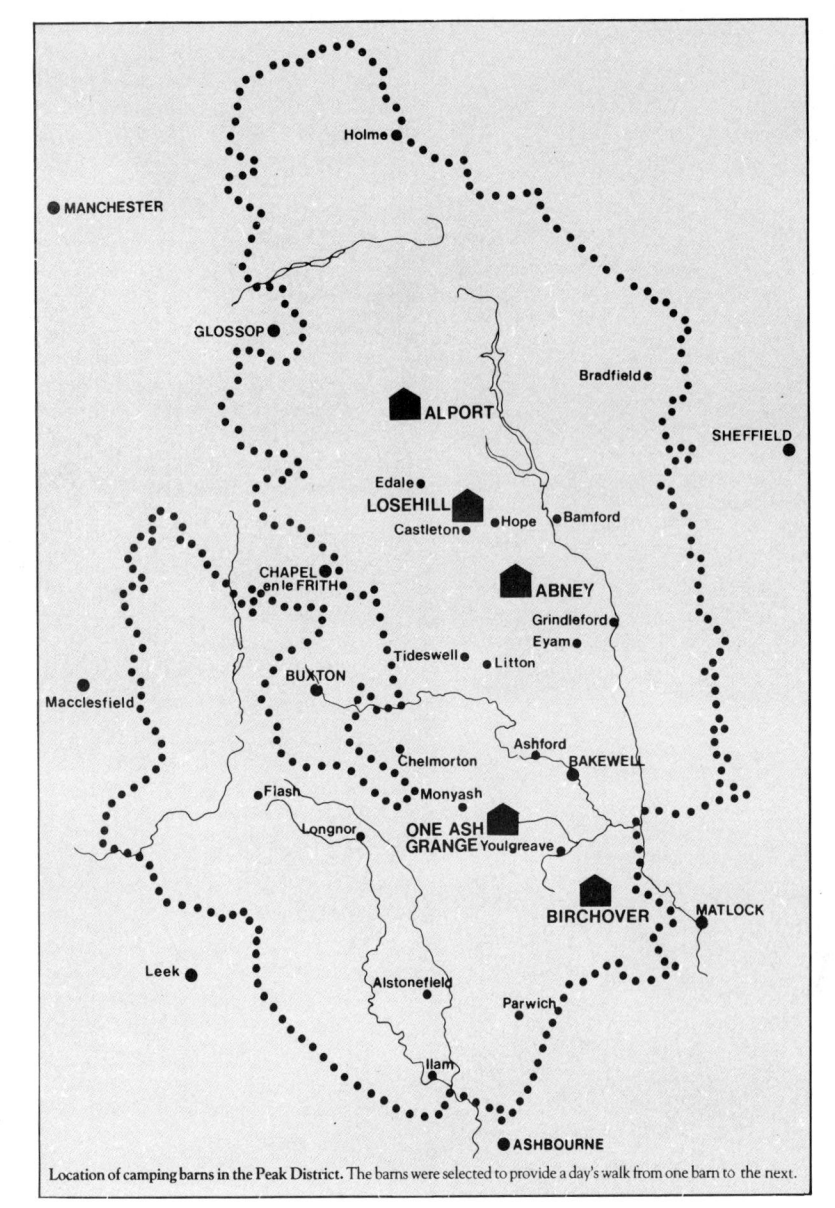

Location of camping barns in the Peak District. The barns were selected to provide a day's walk from one barn to the next.

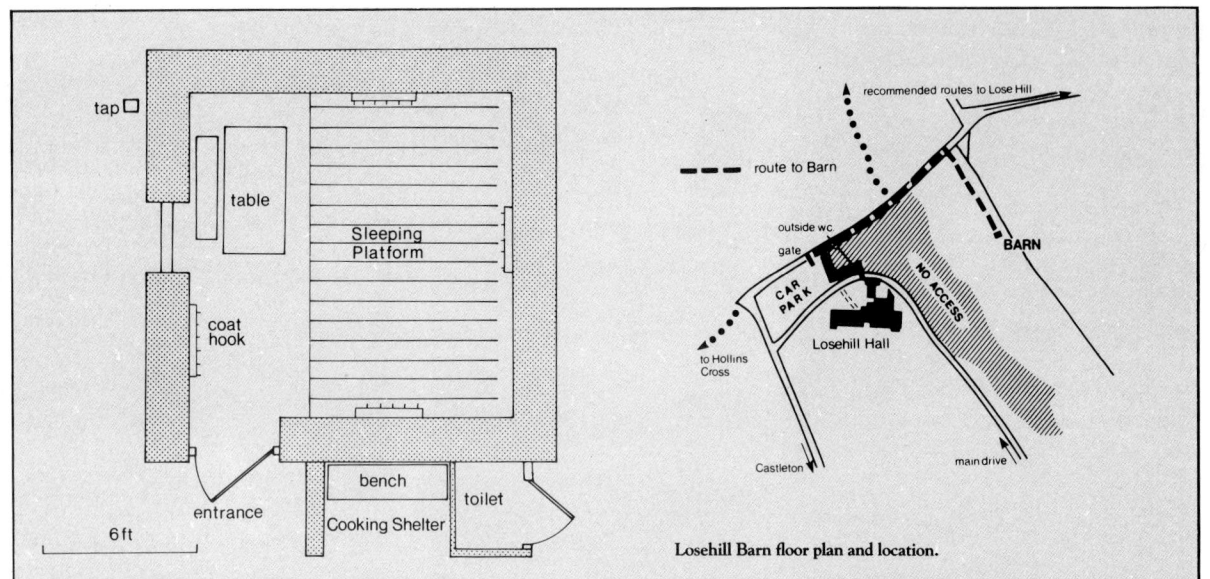

Losehill Barn floor plan and location.

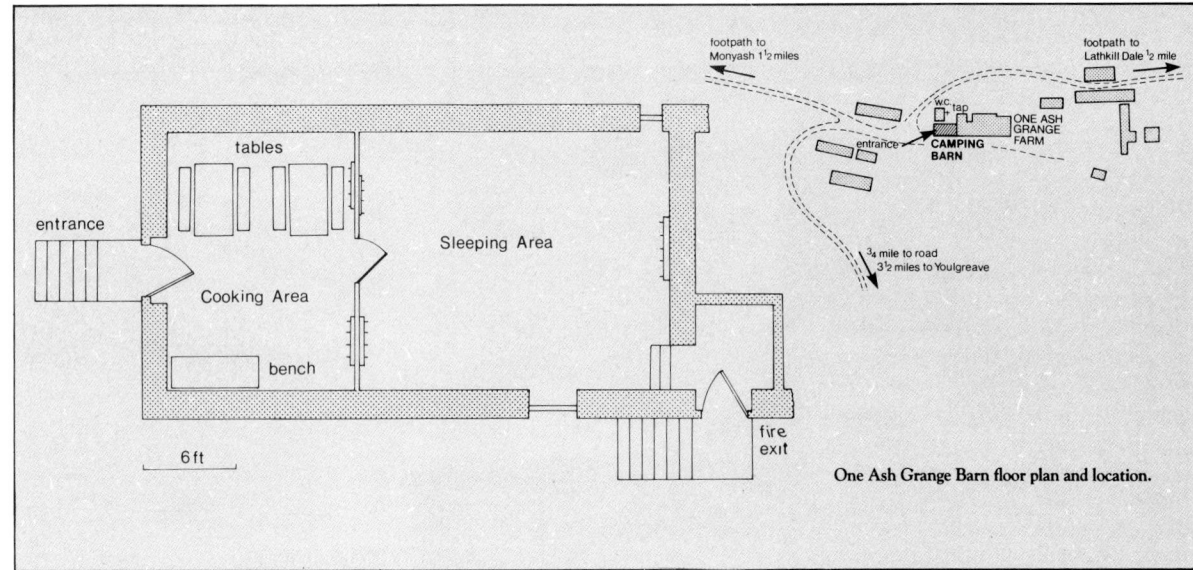

One Ash Grange Barn floor plan and location.

in the Yorkshire Dales, "such an enterprise could indeed produce revenue for the barn operators, often of a significant amount, provided the capital costs could be met". The Peak experiment refers to 'camping barns' rather than 'bunkhouse barns' to underline their more spartan nature. They are often more isolated and costs have been kept to the minimum. In the Dales the farmer or operator has to deal with their own bookings and promotion, whilst the Peak experiment offers a central booking and marketing service to the farmer. The idea was to offer a chain of barns, within walking distance of one another, and the project was for five. For the owners, a typical response was "it's gone much better than I expected", and compared favourably with the amount of work in managing holiday cottages – constantly in need of redecorating as well as thorough cleaning once a week. In this experiment the Countryside Commission contributed about 82% of the conversion costs, but in future the grant aid should come to the farmer through MAFF's farm diversification grant scheme. A second report, on the conversion of four barns in the Yorkshire Dales and North York Moors was produced later in the same year, 1986. Peter Ashcroft, at the Countryside Commission reckons that the current total of camping barns is about twenty, including those in Norfolk and Wales.

So successful has this idea been, that the Countryside Commission has gone into partnership with the Youth Hostels Association, setting up an agency to promote the idea, assist the farmer with planning permissions and grant applications and market the end result. This began in spring this year (1988) and the target is to renovate around seventy-five barns in the next five years. The agency will take the onus from the farmer, and with the experience gained through the conversions already carried out facilitate the process and broaden the experiment. It is to be hoped that the early problems with fire requirements and building regulations will have been ironed out by experience and precedent. Countryside Commission grant aid will still be available for help with barns which do not belong to farmers.

In Northumberland, a corner of a working farmstead at Kirkwhelpington has been converted to provide facilities for campers. It is proof that partial conversion can be perfectly compatible with continuing farming enterprise. It received a CLA commendation for the northern region in 1985.

An unusual solution for remote barns in an area without potential for walkers' shelters or similar has been devised in Oxfordshire. Two listed barns on the Phillimore estate, at Binfield Heath, sited out in the middle of the fields and at the end of a mile-long

ABOVE; Cam Houses Barn, Buckden, North Yorkshire. This is a good example of the Countryside Commission's programme of encouraging the conversion of upland barns to bunkhouses. Early projects were grant-aided by the Countryside Commission and the success of the programme has led to its expansion, with grant aid now coming from MAFF under the farm diversification grant scheme. The conversion of the barn as overnight accommodation for walkers (often school parties) cost only £10,000 (in 1979). It is well located on the Dales Way. Further such conversions are planned within the National Park.

BELOW; Catholes Barn, Sedbergh, Cumbria. The cost of this basic conversion was again around £10,000 and the barn now accommodates 15 walkers. The Countryside Commission has now formed a partnership with the Youth Hostels Association to promote more such conversions. It hopes to convert some 75 barns in the next five years.

Llangoffan Farm, Castle Morris, Dyfed. This former cowshed has become a traditional cheese factory, a remarkable example of new rural industry appropriately located in an old building. Such industries – in effect revivals of old crafts – often seek to locate in such buildings and find them attractive in marketing and "image" building terms. Llangoffan Farmhouse Cheese, founded by a former professional musician, now produces 17,000 lbs. of cheese a year. The conversion of the former cowshed was given a substantial grant by the Welsh Development Agency.

track, are to be repaired and put into use for general purposes in connection with a large shoot. Grain supplies will be stored there and they will provide shelter and storage for syndicate members and gamekeeping staff.

The most common building type after the barn is the cattle shed, or whatever it is called in the numerous regional variations (the vernacular) of the term. Here the buildings are single storeyed, often subdivided, and grouped around a courtyard. This makes them suitable for a related use, kennels or stables, for example, as well as for a grouping of starter workshops or light industrial units, possibly sharing services and amenities. More common, to date, has been the conversion of these ranges of buildings to holiday accommodation, since they are common in areas of high tourist attraction such as Devon or north Norfolk. In some respects they suit the use since their inward facing aspect can leave the outer walls relatively unaltered. On the other hand, over-supply has begun to drench the market and planning authorities are beginning to be wary of further applications, favouring those which ensure permanent occupation. A model, in terms of the self-effacing way in which it has been converted by the National Trust are the range of farm buildings at Stackpole, in Pembroke where the domestic aspects are entirely confined to the internal courtyard.

A novel use for a range of similar stocksheds, this time in Clackmannan, Scotland, was the conversion to a small brewery, Harviestoun 'established 1983'. The brewery is on a working farm, and the farmer buys the spent grain to feed his sheep. Mr. Brooker, who founded the brewery was strongly encouraged "to start in a new, prefabricated building on an industrial site but knew that the character of this building was exactly what a brewery should be . . . I feature the building in the leaflet . . . it portrays the traditional image that people expect a brewery to have so I consider it is good promotionally".

For very much the same reason a number of manufacturers of successful dairy products, cheeses, yoghurts and ice-creams make a point of working out of traditional buildings. One such is the much-praised Llangloffan Farmhouse Cheese enterprise, at Castle Morris, Pembroke, where a single storey cowshed is used for a small milking parlour, cooling room, cheese-making room, cheese-press room and a cheese store. From here Leon Downey (previously co-principal viola player in the Halle Orchestra) produces 17,000 lbs. of cheese a year. Of conversion costs of around £30,000, 35% came from the Welsh Development Agency. With the current boom in farmhouse made products, particularly those made from dairy products, many cowsheds and dairy buildings have found a new and productive use. After all, if a proportion of purchases are made on the spot, in a farm shop, the character of the farm is not insignificant in marketing terms. Use of old buildings identifies with a traditional image, upon which much of this market depends. Such successes in preserves and pickles, other dairy products, dried herbs and so on, have extended the ideas of 'on-farm processing and sale' – an extension of the farm shop which augurs well for the historic farmstead.

Equally, with changes in farm policy

FAR LEFT; Stackpole Farm, Dyfed. The arrangement of these farm buildings around a courtyard makes a variety of new uses possible. Holiday accommodation is certainly one appropriate use, though in some areas, including Pembrokeshire, local authorities are anxious to limit the spread of holiday homes.

LEFT; Harvieston Brewery, Clackmannan, Scotland. This is another example of a traditional craft revived in a former farm building. A range of redundant stock-sheds, part of a working farm, was sold to the new brewery in 1983.

BELOW; Lower Treginnis Farm, near St. David's, Dyfed. This farm group is the subject of a collaboration between the National Trust and Farms for City Children. The farm is still operative, and will remain so. The foldyard, however, will, be converted to provide a residential educational complex.

it may well be quicker and more expedient to convert existing buildings if, as in the case of a Suffolk farm at Thurston, the farm is utilising surplus milk, here as icecream. The delays in designing and fabricating a purpose-built structure are liable to be longer, and probably more expensive, than a relatively straight-forward conversion of a building already standing on the site. CoSIRA provides cosings which prove in some cases, how economic, re-use can be.

A pair of weather-boarded, timber framed barns on the Wormsley Estate, near Watlington in Oxfordshire, have been beautifully converted into storage space and accommodation for the estate timber yards. Sufficiently large to house equipment, with a small linking building which provides a lunch 'hut' and toilets, it gives the lie to the inadequacy of traditional farm buildings for new, rural industries. In particular at a time when forestry and woodland management are becoming an important arm in the MAFF push for diversification, this is a particularly good example that many farmers or land owners with a redundant threshing barn or two might follow. The work was carried out by surveyors with Strutt & Parker who as agents to many large estates are in an ideal position to use this as an example of what may be done.

Although most examples of conversion tend to be individual buildings, or ranges of buildings, there are also schemes which involve either an entire farmstead or a model farm as such. Farms for City Children project started twelve years ago, on a farm at Nethercott House in Devon. Now the success of that project, and the inevitable limits on the number of children who can visit within a year, has led to a link-up between the National Trust and Farms for City Children. Lower Treginnis, St. Davids comprises a variety of traditional buildings grouped around the farmhouse. Most of these will remain in use but the main foldyard will be converted to provide

Former Stockyard, Pilsley, Derbyshire. The Chatsworth Estate has been extremely conscientious about the fate of its redundant farm buildings and some excellent conversions have resulted. At Pilsley, the large stockyard complex houses both an estate shop and some workshops let to small industries. The conversion has been done with sensitivity and taste, with the new elements skilfully slotted in and kept to a minimum. The temptation to "folksiness' has been resisted.

BELOW; Amongst the new businesses now based at Pilsley is a picture framers. The obvious use for buildings of this sort is as residential accommodation, but commercial and light industrial use now involves less change to the buildings and can contribute significantly to the local economy. Farm and estate shops are now very profitable enterprises. The location of this example at Pilsley, in a former farm building, is an important part of its appeal.

a dormitory, library, kitchen and dining room as well as a 'quiet room' and a 'rumpus room'. At a cost of approaching £500,000 this is clearly an exceptional use because of its scale and complexity, but equally it suggests the educational potential for the farm, from Farm Trails to more specialised link-ups with schools or higher education establishments.

The remarkable success story of the Lockinge Trust is, by now, well known but the gradual conversion of a number of Victorian farm buildings, including a hay barn, cow shed, dairy, cart horse stabling, calf shed, loose boxes, calving boxes and bull boxes, has added further light industrial and craft units to what is virtually a rural industrial estate. It has all led to a remarkable revival in the fortunes of a group of villages near Wantage – to the extent that the benefits are now extending to the provision of fair rented accommodation and increased security for all the existing village amenities, including a village school.

It is an example of the 'knock-on' effect that a small enterprise, quite possibly housed in converted farm buildings, can have on an entire community.

Although the present success has taken fifteen years to achieve, it was based upon discussions with CoSIRA beginning in 1973, and was facilitated

Wroxham, Norfolk. This group of brick-built barns and stock sheds is one of the best conversions in East Anglia. The uses are very varied, including shops, a café, and a craft gallery. Crafts centres are obvious uses for redundant farm buildings but many have failed within a relatively short space. This example has prospered, and the scheme (grant aided by CoSIRA) is respectful of the buildings.

by the eagerness and initiative of the Loyd Estate to put new life back into an established, but dwindling, rural community.

Another estate which has been unremittingly conscientious about the future of its architecture has been Chatsworth; the conversion of a stockyard complex at Pilsley into a farm shop and four separate workshops is a good example of how well-suited a courtyard type design is for such units – despite the more usual choice of residential conversion. A group of brick barns and stock sheds at Wroxham, Norfolk, a CLA/CoSIRA competition winner in 1984, is another such conversion, within buildings of different materials and different character.

After the barn and the cattle shed, there are numerous purpose-built structures which tend to reflect the agricultural developments of the 18th and 19th centuries. Oast houses, developed from the kiln, are one such local variation. In Hampshire a range of oasts have been converted to ten starter industrial units.

Cartsheds, usually arcaded, with a secure granary overhead, are often still in use for storage, while the detached granary can be used as a store and is sufficiently small to not be a great drain on resources. Dovecotes, of ancient and manorial derivation,

THIS PAGE; Model Farm at Easton, Suffolk: now a farm museum.
OPPOSITE PAGE; Tithe Barn, Titchfield, Hampshire. This has now been converted into a very successful farm shop.
OPPOSITE PAGE, ABOVE AND BELOW; A barn at Farley Green, Surrey, has been converted into a church without the need for much alteration.

are also among the category of small and specialist buildings – hardly suitable for conversion although a luxury hotel in Oxfordshire is planning to turn theirs into a separate room for guests.

The lists are not comprehensive guides to the best traditional farm buildings but most architect designed or model farms are better recognised, recorded and generally listed. In some cases the model farm has been turned, in its entirety into a farm park. Easton in Suffolk is one example, with various displays housed in barns and cattle sheds, with the Victorian model dairy as the *pièce de résistance* in the middle of the site. Home Farm, Shipley Park is another example, a complex designed in 1860 by William Eden Nesfield. Described as a 'traditional farming holiday and educational centre' it encourages children to participate in traditional farm tasks, such as milking, feeding and mucking out. The buildings grouped in a courtyard are ornamented by a 'baronial style' dovecote and an octagonal dairy.

A range of model farm buildings on the Escot estate in Devon have been converted into an ambitious enterprise breeding ornamental fish. Starting with grants from CoSIRA and additional finance from a merchant bank, J. Kennaway has diversified his business year by year. Pig sties have become fish tanks, tractor sheds house aquaria and the Koi carp live in the cow stalls. To accommodate the

JOE LOW

ROD WILD

ROD WILD

77

public, stable blocks are now being converted to tea-rooms and a restaurant, this time with grant aid from the regional Tourist Board. The arcaded model farm buildings are used as the retail centre.

A range of banded brick, Victorian farm buildings on the outskirts of Dunmow have been converted to five individual workshop units, including a boat building business, metal fabrication and hospital equipment manufacturers. The conversion has provided jobs for twenty people and left the building virtually unaltered from the exterior. A late Victorian model farm, included within Washington New Town, has become Biddick Farm Arts Centre. The works were phased and carried out by the architects' department of the New Town. A number of other farms which have found themselves within the boundaries of New or Expanded Towns, such as Northampton or Milton Keynes have found new uses as community centres or general amenities for arts and recreation within the town.

OPPOSITE PAGE; Biddick Farm Arts Centre, Washington, Tyne and Wear. This farm complex near to Fatfield village centre has been converted to provide a 130 seat theatre (illustrated here), together with an art gallery, craft workshops, two residential units and a community meeting room for village residents. The scheme was carried out as a phased development between 1973 and 1977 by the Washington Development Corporation.

THIS PAGE; Barns on the Wormsley Estate, near Watlington, Oxfordshire. Traditional barns are being carefully restored to provide accommodation for various activities carried out on the estate. The barn (ABOVE RIGHT) was in a similar condition to that illustrated on the left. It has now been fully restored using traditional materials and has become the centre of the estate's large forestry enterprise. The scheme won a CLA award last year. Now the two other complexes of barns on the estate are being restored in order to provide the estate with much needed workshop space.

JOE LOW

OPPOSITE PAGE; Wormsley Estate, near Watlington, Oxfordshire. As part of the restoration of the award winning barn shown (ABOVE RIGHT) . . . on the previous page, the stables have been repaired and will soon house horses again. Much of the beech woodland is on steep chalk slopes and the use of heavy machinery for logging was causing serious soil erosion. The estate are therefore introducing horses to do the work as a practical and economic alternative.

THIS PAGE; Home Farm, Lockinge Estate, near Wantage, Oxfordshire. A range of farm buildings converted to workshops create a lively complex in the village. The Ardington Pottery (ABOVE), run by Les and Brenda Owens, occupies the picturesque old dairy. Michael Eastham restores church monuments and statuary, (BELOW), in the old barn and finds the original large doors ideal for manoeuvring substantial and immensely heavy pieces of stonework. Nutwood Toys, (CENTRE), have recently taken space in the complex. They set up their business with help from CoSIRA and make colourful handmade wooden toys. A restorer of pine furniture, (LEFT), joinery workshop, chair recaning business, forge and other enterprises are housed in the scheme.

Maiden Newton, Dorset. Typical medieval barn built beside its church.

SUMMARY AND CONCLUSIONS

GOVERNMENT AND GOVERNMENT AGENCIES MUST

- present a coherent policy.

- recognise the enormous regional differences, which affect policy, grant aid and development control.

- ensure that information on legislation and grant aid is accessible and comprehensible.

- ensure that such aid is available with the minimum of bureaucratic delay.

- ensure, in the case of listed buildings, that the maximum effort is made to retain the building with as little alteration to its fabric, external and internal, as is feasible.

- correct an imbalance between the funding for conservation and economic development in urban and rural areas.

- increase the resources available for grant aid to listed buildings.

- remove or reduce the imposition of VAT on historic buildings.

- develop and implement ideas such as that of "Rural Conservation Areas" or "Rural Town Schemes".

- strengthen the role and the funding of the Rural Development Commission.

- provide support for planning authorities (the enormous increase in successful appeals against planning decisions is a worrying development).

- promote properly supervised job creation schemes and Community Programmes which involve the repair of traditional farm buildings.

- change the procedure for listed building consent to include the submission of detailed drawings regarding building regulations at the first stage, by which the applicant must abide, or re-apply with new drawings.

LOCAL AUTHORITIES MUST

- offer information and guidance to applicants, in the best interests of the building.

- publicise the potential wide range of uses, funding, etc. (as, for example, in the form of travelling exhibitions).

- know the extent of the issue: computerisation of records, keeping buildings at risk registers.

- realise that such information can also help to solve the problem by matching buildings to potential tenants.

- be aware of the risk of changes between submission for outline planning permission and the outcome.

- ensure that councillors are well informed of the issues.

- develop non-statutory local plans on the topic of redundant farm buildings, conversion and re-use.

- tread warily in providing Design Guides for residential conversion which tend to become blueprints for applicants.

- be aware that where a listed farm building has been ruined by poor conversion de-listing is likely.

- use their statutory powers to prosecute where abuses have occurred.

LOCAL COMMUNITY: PARISH COUNCILS, AMENITY SOCIETIES, BUILDING PRESERVATION TRUSTS, MUST

- be aware of the scale of the problem of bad and inappropriate conversions.

- intervene at the proper moment in the planning process and ensure that their comments are informed and deal with planning issues, rather than raising subjective objections.

- consider the possibility of community use for a suitably located redundant barn (village hall, sports facility, etc., uses which can attract considerable grant aid from the appropriate body).

- learn from the example of campaigns mounted by the natural landscape conservation lobby (far more successful in presenting the case for rural issues than the lobby for the rural built environment).

- initiate local award schemes to encourage better quality conversions.

- aim to carry out exemplary schemes as an encouragement to others with particular attention to the simple details which affect character, too often ignored or misunderstood in poor conversions.

FARMERS AND LANDOWNERS MUST

- consider their traditional farm buildings first and foremost as a potential resource within agriculture.

- think long-term. A quick capital return on a residential conversion may be less attractive than investment in conversion to light industrial or workshop space, paying dividends over an indefinite period.

- be wary of the developer who offers them a sum for a redundant farm building, which then appears for sale with outline planning permission, for a greatly increased sum.

- remember the intangible benefits of a built landscape in good order, if they hope to attract visitors to their farm or area.

- consider farm buildings as a potential resource when they are diversifying.

- remember the advantages of traditional accommodation for, for instance, animal husbandry.

- consider the advantages of low cost constant maintenance of an existing barn or farm building over the capital costs of a new structure, which may itself be shortly redundant.

- remember the importance of image in farm-based enterprise; cheese-making or a farm shop in traditional premises are far more appealing to tourists in such a setting than in the equivalent to a factory on a new industrial estate.

- co-operate with neighbouring farmers in ventures which may well suggest a use for a disused farm building.

DEVELOPERS AND NON-FARMING OWNERS MUST

- consider the suitability of the building and its location to the intended new use.

- be aware of the planning authority standpoint and possible strong objection on conversion, particularly to residential use.

- realise that the costs of high quality conversion on a listed building may make the development considerably less profitable than they might imagine.

- realise that a well designed and appropriate conversion is more likely to get planning permission speedily, which saves time and money.

BIBLIOGRAPHY

British Tourist Authority, *Britain's Historic Buildings: A Policy for their Future Use,* 1980, (The Montagu Report).

Brunskill, R. W., *Illustrated Handbook of Vernacular Architecture,* 1971 and revised later editions.

Brunskill, R. W., *Traditional Farm Buildings of Britain,* new edition 1987.

Country Landowners' Association, *The Gretton Report,* 1985.

Countryside Commission, *The Use and Management of Bunkhouse Barns,* 1986.

Countryside Commission, *Camping Barns in the Peak District,* 1986.

Cunnington, Pamela, *Change of Use: The Conversion of Old Buildings,* 1988.

Darley, Gillian, *The National Trust Book of the Farm,* 1981.

English Heritage, *Directory of Public Sources of Grants for the Repair and Conversion of Historic Buildings,* 1988 (looseleaf, to allow for regular amendments and additions).

Essex County Council, *Historic Barns: A Planning Appraisal,* 1979.

Essex County Council, *Historic Buildings at Risk,* 1987/8, (Part 2: Agricultural Structures).

Hampshire County Council, *Saving Old Farm Buildings,* 1982.

Harvey, Nigel, *A History of Farm Buildings in England and Wales,* revised, 1984.

HMSO, *Farming and Rural Enterprise* (information pack), 1987.

Hughes, Graham, *Barns of Rural Britain,* 1985.

Historic Farm Buildings Group *Journal,* 1987.

National Farmers' Union, *Redundant Farm Buildings,* T. Horsefield, 1988.

Norfolk County Council, *Historic Buildings in Norfolk: Problems and Opportunities,* 1987.

Rural Voice, *A Rural Strategy,* 1987.

SAVE Britain's Heritage, *Conservation: A Credit Account,* Michael Pearce, 1988.

Society for the Protection of Ancient Buildings, *Barns Book* (Conference Report), 1982.

Society for the Protection of Ancient Buildings, *First Aid Repair to Traditional Farm Buildings,* John Sell.

Weller, John, *History of the Farmstead,* 1982.

Wild, Rod, *Surrey Barn Survey,* 1988.

Wilkinson, Pauline, *Redundant Farm Buildings: Alternative Uses in the Remoter Rural Areas of England and Wales,* College of Estate Management, Centre for Advanced Land Use Studies, University of Reading, 1987.

Woodfoorde, John, *Farm Buildings,* 1983.

FRONT COVER; Traditional farm buildings in a Norfolk village.
BACK COVER; Detail of chalk and flint barn in The Thames Valley.
PAGE ONE; Detail of brick barn gable end in Norfolk.
PAGE THREE; Coombeshead Farm, Arlington, Devon.